Mindfulness and Intimacy

MINDFULNESS AND INTIMACY

Ben Connelly

Wisdom Publications
199 Elm Street
Somerville, MA 02144 USA
wisdompubs.org

Library of Congress Cataloging-in-Publication Data
Names: Connelly, Ben, author.
Title: Mindfulness and intimacy / Ben Connelly.
Description: Somerville, MA: Wisdom Publications, [2019] | Includes bibliographical references. |
Identifiers: LCCN 2018020827 (print) | LCCN 2018042102 (ebook) | ISBN 9781614295167 (e-book) | ISBN 9781614294962 (pbk.: alk. paper)
Subjects: LCSH: Meditation—Buddhism. | Awareness—Religious aspects—Buddhism—Meditations. | Consciousness—Religious aspects—Buddhism—Meditations. | Intimacy (Psychology)—Religious aspects—Buddhism—Meditations.
Classification: LCC BQ5612 (ebook) | LCC BQ5612 .C66 2018 (print) | DDC 294.3/4435—dc23
LC record available at https://lccn.loc.gov/2018020827

ISBN 978-1-61429-496-2   ebook ISBN 978-1-61429-516-7

23 22 21 20 19   5 4 3 2 1

Cover design by Phil Pascuzzo. Interior design by Gopa&Ted 2; typeset by Tony Lulek. Set in Requiem 10.9/15.8.

♲ Wisdom Publications' books are printed on acid-free paper and meet the guidelines for permanence and durability of the Production Guidelines for Book Longevity of the Council on Library Resources.

This book was produced with environmental mindfulness.
For more information, please visit wisdompubs.org/wisdom-environment.

Printed in the United States of America.

Please visit fscus.org.

As I write near the shores of Bde Maka Ska,
I honor and thank the Dakota and Ojibwe people
for their long and continued care
for the lands that I call home.

Table of Contents

List of Practices

Introduction

Here we are, together through words, and also through infinite connections that are beyond our capacity to conceive. Aware of these words right now, we are intimate in our mindfulness of just this reading and just this writing. We all have some sense of how to be mindful, to be focused on what's here in the present moment, and we all have some sense of how to be intimate, to be connected, to realize the depth of our relationship to someone or something. We may also have some sense of how this mindfulness and intimacy can promote a joyful life based on compassionate engagement with what is right here and now. This book is an opportunity to deepen this understanding and to deepen our capacity to experience this mindfulness and intimacy, for these can be cultivated through practice.

Mindfulness has deep roots in the Buddhist tradition. These days it is also very popular with people in many secular and non-Buddhist religious contexts. The majority of my training on the subject has been as a Zen teacher, and I will draw extensively on teachings from the Buddhist canon in this book. I will also draw on literature from science, other religions, and secular traditions. This practice, and what I will be encouraging, does not require any particular set of beliefs. If you practice Zen, Tibetan, or Vipassana Buddhism, this book is for you. If you are Muslim, Christian, Jewish, or of some other religious persuasion, these teachings can benefit your life and complement your religious practice. If you are nonreligious, you can do these practices just as well as any religious person.

Intimacy means "closeness" or "friendship." It is a very deep and powerful aspect of our lives. Many of us have known the towering heights of an early romantic attachment. And all of us sadly will know the wrenching grief of the loss of those we love—and of our own lives. Though intimacy includes and calls up all our strongest emotions, we can learn to meet it with equanimity, with compassion; we can realize intimacy as a way to go directly toward what is deepest and most powerful about being human. We, all people, and all things are already interdependent, intimately connected, and as Martin Luther King Jr. wrote, "tied in a single garment of destiny." We can cultivate our awareness of this intimacy with everything and everyone we experience: our bodies, our minds, our families, our lovers, the natural world, our communities, our environment, and more. Thus we can open a path toward a more conscious and intentional engagement with both the joys and sorrows of our daily lives, our families, our political world, and our planet.

As a person of European descent with a middle-class upbringing, I carry a perspective formed by many privileges. I have tried to hear the voices of living people from many cultures and backgrounds to inform this writing. I have also called on thousands of years of writings about the transformative power of mindfulness and intimacy. This power has been recounted in the stories of the lives of a dazzlingly diverse array of people of many different cultures and ethnicities: queens, servants, merchants, farmers, sex workers, healers, teachers, warriors, artists, the blind and the sighted, the old, the young, the sick and the hale, the rich and the poor, the cruel and foolish, and the very wise. These are stories of empowerment, but not of a power that is given from one to another—a liberative power we each already have.

Throughout this book I will provide specific practices you can take up to cultivate mindfulness and intimacy within the many aspects of life. If you simply read this book and don't do any of the practices, that's just fine. However, if you find that the material in the book rings true to you, doing the practices is a great opportunity to bring it to life, to experience it in a deep and personal way. There are few things more empowering and joyful than choosing a life based on your own values and what is in front of you right now. I hope this book helps you, through intimacy with yourself, to deepen your connection to your heart and the whole great world, and through mindfulness, to deepen your connection to what's right here.

1. Mindfulness

Mindfulness is being aware of things in the present moment in a way that promotes well-being. To practice mindfulness is to choose some aspect of our experience and focus attention there in a sustained way. There is discernment in mindfulness, but it is nonjudgmental; it is kind. It allows the mind to rest in the phenomena of the present moment and take a break from creating a relentless stream of imaginations about the future, reviews of the past, or judgments of the present. Our awareness is one of the most amazing and powerful things we have as human beings. Rather than taking it for granted and allowing it to focus wherever the mind's habits choose, with mindfulness we can better focus awareness on things that are truly beneficial.

I recall finding myself up on a ladder last summer painting my garage. It was very hot; there were lots of buzzing flies. I was irritable, thinking about how unpleasant it all was. Looking through sweat-burned eyes at the amount of unpainted wall remaining, I calculated just how long it would take before I could be done. I made this calculation several times, impatient, and then I remembered the value of mindfulness, of focusing first on the sensations in my body and emotions, and then focusing completely on the task at hand. I noticed my feet, a bit sore from the narrow rungs of the ladder, the heat of the body in the sun, the cranky feeling. I just offered awareness to those feelings—I didn't ask them to leave or try to avoid them—and I felt a little more calm. So I turned to really noticing what this painting was like: the smooth, slick wetness of the yellow paint as it covered the cracked white stain, the heft of the brush in the hand as it came up from the can. Every stroke of the brush produced a unique and glistening pattern on the wall, and all around I saw the wetness fading and the dry paint's matte warmth taking hold. It was very pleasant. I can see the garage out the window now; it looks well taken care of. Understanding how to focus our awareness, how to practice mindfulness, can help us shed unpleasant emotional states and habits of thought—and can help us take care of things.

With mindfulness we can become aware of aspects of our experience that are normally unconscious. We can begin to notice tensions and relaxations, energy and lassitude in the body that are always with us, but which we usually ignore. We can be aware of the quality of our breath, which reflects our emotions and mind. We can become aware of how we feel. We can see the thoughts that drive us not as true stories but simply as something that is happening, like the sound of the birds outside my window. One of the first and most powerful steps in mindfulness practice is to bring the unconscious elements of what we think we are into the light of awareness.

Mindfulness is a translation of an ancient word from India, *smrti*. *Smrti* is sometimes translated as "remembering," or "calling to mind." When I was painting the garage I had to remember to pay attention. I had to call to mind the elements of experience that would help me be well. Otherwise I might have just remained in my mind's trance about how life would be better once I got finished. These days most of us associate mindfulness with attention to the breath, a task, or perhaps the natural world. However, the foundational text on mindfulness practice, the Buddhist *Four Foundations of Mindfulness Sutra* (*Satipatthana Sutta*), also includes practices of focusing the mind on specific thoughts and images, particularly ones associated with death. The early Buddhist practice of mindfulness of death can help us to remember, or call to mind, the value of this fleeting opportunity we have in each moment to be well and to practice in order to promote wellness.

Here in the early part of the twenty-first century, mindfulness has become widely known in the Western world. In the last fifty years, people trained in Buddhism began adapting the practice to secular contexts, and mountains of science has emerged showing the health and wellness benefits of the practice. The meaning of the word *mindfulness* has broadened, and nowadays when I'm going through the checkout line at the grocery store I often see a few "mindful coloring books" on sale. I haven't actually tried mindful coloring, but it sounds like it might be soothing, not so different than painting a garage. However, it's quite a ways from the practices laid out in the *Four Foundations of Mindfulness Sutra*. Words and practices evolve, and this is natural and good. The teachings in this book, though, will be deeply rooted in techniques practiced for thousands of years. This book will help us to cultivate the four foundations (mindfulness of body, feeling, mind, and phenomena) in roughly the same sequence as the original teachings, first focusing our awareness on the body and those things we think of as "self," and slowly expanding to a broader and more expansive awareness.

Holistic (or right) mindfulness is the seventh element of the Buddhist eightfold path: holistic view, intention, speech, action, livelihood, effort, mindfulness, and meditative absorption. It is a key element to the path to nonsuffering, which is the heart of all Buddhist teachings. This eightfold path can be summed up thus: making a commitment to alleviating suffering through compassionate living and meditation. You don't have to be of any particular religious persuasion to see the beauty in that, or to do it. Mindfulness is sometimes understood to be a meditation practice, but we can learn to carry mindfulness throughout our lives and allow it to infuse all our actions, at work or at play, with compassion, with kind awareness of things right now. You will find that throughout this book I offer mindfulness practices that are intended to help us cultivate a life of kind engagement with the world. This is the kind of life where we find the deepest meaning and sense of personal well-being.

Mindfulness is cooling and calming. The early Buddhist teachings where mindfulness is most central emphasize dispassion, letting go of intense emotions, letting go of attachments. Over the last forty years psychologists and neuroscientists who were also trained in Buddhist meditation have been demonstrating how effective it is at alleviating suffering and promoting wellness. A wide array of psychological systems and acronyms—such as MBSR, MBCT, ACT, DBT, MDT, and Morita therapy—have been developed to access its efficacy. Early Buddhist teachings integrate mindfulness, ethical living, and deep meditation to help people attain nirvana, a state of being cooled, with the fires of suffering and intense emotion blown out. Mindfulness can help us settle down into a calm, nonreactive relationship with how things are. It can help us find peace in every step, in every word, in every drop of rain we hear against our windowpane. But mindfulness without some cultivation of compassionate living and awareness of interdependence—without intimacy—is too dry. Early Buddhist teachings always paired mindfulness with these other elements of practice. And the later Mahayana school of Buddhism actively deemphasized mindfulness and focused on interdependence, on intimacy, because it felt that rather than focusing on the sound of the rain on the window it was more important to step outside into the rain, jump in a few puddles, help some elderly folks get their umbrellas open, and invite some folks without umbrellas to join us under ours. If we don't realize our intimacy, our mindfulness may help us to be cool, calm observers, but it will not really open us up to the deep, wide, wild river of life, to just how vast and amazing each moment can be.

2. Intimacy

Intimacy in its simplest definition means close familiarity and friendship. Words, however, have power and meaning beyond their definitions. No matter what the dictionary says, some words evoke very different meanings or feelings to different people. To some folks the word *religion* evokes inspiration, warmth, and wonder, to others constriction and closed-mindedness. *Intimacy* is a word a bit like this. It can evoke feelings of connection and safety, but for some people it's pretty scary, or stickily sentimental. And then there are the folks who think it just means sex. Here I will be pointing toward a way of understanding and experiencing the word *intimacy* that fosters compassion, calm, and joyful action. I use *intimacy* here as we often use it in Zen discourse; it's about harmony between autonomy and interdependence. In intimacy we are individuals who are connected, and we are also one undivided whole; we can develop both healthy boundaries and healthy boundarylessness.

I invite you to take a moment to reflect on the most healthy, rewarding, intimate relationship you've known. Notice how thinking about it makes you feel. For some of us, intimate relationships have been so fraught throughout our lives that this kind of recollection is quite painful. For others of us the list of wonderful relationships is so long we can't decide which one to focus on. No matter where you fall on this spectrum, you can use what you know and feel about intimacy to deepen your ability to connect on a profound level to yourself, to other people, and to the entire world. Your feeling about intimacy is a reflection of what intimacy is about: it's your feeling right now, personal and immediate, and it is the result of infinite conditions and is connected to everything that will ever happen.

Human consciousness has evolved so that we experience life from a position of alienation. We generally feel like we exist as beings separate from the rest of the universe. We walk down the street and it seems as if we are an awareness bobbing around on top of a body, perceiving a bunch of things outside ourselves: trees, bikes, cars, dog barks, graffiti. We listen to others talking and sometimes we understand them and sometimes we don't, but they always seem separate from us on some level.

Buddhist teachings, and mystic teachings from many other religions, have long focused on helping us let go of the habit of feeling like we are separate from everything. They provide practices to help us realize, to experientially know, that we are in fact a part—or not even separate enough to be a part—of a vast, ever-unfolding whole. The reason is simple: people who let go of this habit of alienation report a sense of oceanic peace and well-being and tend to devote themselves to lots of compassionate actions for those around them. Many neuroscientists say that our sense of being a separate, persistent self is just a construct of the processes in our brain.

Regardless of what all these experts say, it still seems like I'm typing, and I suspect that you sense that it is a real, separate you that is reading right now.

The practice and cultivation of intimacy is not ultimately about eliminating or getting rid of this sense that we are apart from the world. Since intimacy is about harmonizing autonomy and interdependence, what we really need to do is get our sense of separateness in balance with our sense of connection. Many spiritual teachings see us as so out of balance in this regard that they use very powerful rhetoric to get us to let go of the alienated position of separation and open up to the infinite. The Koran, for instance, says that Allah is "closer than your jugular vein," and the great Christian mystic Meister Eckhart wrote, "My eye and God's eye are one eye, one knowing, one love." Cracking through the habit of believing we're the bump on the universe generally takes a lot of practice and a lot of support. Meditation is one of the most powerful practices for breaking this habit, but many other things can help, particularly practices that diminish our focus on getting things for ourselves. Self-serving actions tend to harden our sense of separateness; actions based in our sense of intimacy soften it.

In these pages we'll have time to investigate many ways to engage in the world based on our sense of connection: doing simple tasks with altruistic intentions, cultivating kindness with our loved ones and toward ourselves, exploring our capacity to help in the face of huge social problems like racism, sexism, and classism, and harmonizing our lives with the natural world, with ecology and our warming planet. We'll investigate these not with commandments and obligations but by attuning our hearts to our intimacy with things and letting the power of our personal aspirations move us forward.

Mindfulness is an object-based practice: we focus our awareness on a particular thing. In order for there to be an object we must be a subject, separate from it, and observing it. For this reason, it is very common in Mahayana Buddhist literature to critique or downplay the value of mindfulness. Mahayana teachings focus on interdependence, on seeing through the illusion of separateness made by our conceptual mind. They say that if we let the mind settle down enough we will realize that there are no separate things, just a vast, interconnected whole. So they say that an object-based meditation (such as mindfulness) hardens our tendency to see things as objects. They encourage objectless meditation instead: just realizing intimacy with everything right now. This book is about finding a middle way between a total focus on mindfulness practice and a total focus on objectless practice.

In objectless meditation, there is no specific thing on which we try to focus, and there is no goal (or object) of meditation. We just be. We could say that objectless meditation is a nonjudgmental, panoramic awareness of what is happening now—sounds, sights, thoughts, feelings, bodily sensations. If you try objectless meditation without some previous training, it is likely that your mind will just carry you away on a river of ideas about the future or the past. Without some guidance the mind tends to just do what it habitually does. I have a friend, however, who told me an interesting story about objectless meditation. When he was a young boy he studied karate, and at every practice the teacher would proclaim "zazen!" All the students would drop to the mat cross-legged and remain dead still for ten minutes or so. My friend had no idea what this was about, except that he was supposed to sit still. He told me that he didn't learn until he was much older that *zazen* means "sitting meditation" or "sitting Zen" in Japanese. He also told me that after doing it at the karate dojo for years, even though he had no idea why, he found a deep peace and stillness in the practice of just sitting with no sense of purpose or object of concentration.

I suspect that if people came to an "introduction to meditation" class with me and I just said "zazen!" with no other instruction, it wouldn't go all that well. People want a little more guidance in focusing their minds. I usually recommend starting meditation with mindfulness of breathing, and then as the mind settles, perhaps we let it settle into objectless meditation.

Although it is difficult to grasp, there is a deep wisdom in objectless meditation. It is harder to understand and to package than mindfulness, and this may be why we have such a large mindfulness movement these days and there is a lot less talk about the objectless side of meditation.

Although mindfulness practices ask us to focus on an object, they do sometimes invite us to enter into a total, not-separate intimacy with our object of concentration. Object-based meditation is intimately connected to objectless meditation. We will explore their difference and their sameness through practices laid out in the following pages.

These days, mindfulness is big. You can find articles on mindfulness on the covers of all kinds of magazines and write-ups in newspapers. It's in schools and churches, law firms and clinics. When I teach meditation at halfway houses for folks in recovery, I generally ask how many people have had mindfulness training before. Five years ago I'd see a few hands; these days, every hand is in the air. It's wonderful that so many people are finding the benefits of this ancient practice, but without the traditional complements of intimacy-based practices like objectless meditation and working within community, with teachers, and in nature, its power is profoundly limited. Mindfulness paired with intimacy opens up a much deeper and richer possibility for how we can live. Not only can we find all the well-documented health and wellness benefits of mindfulness practice, but we can open up to one of the deepest human joys: love and service, a life of intimate engagement.

3. Self

An old Zen saying goes, "First there is a mountain, then there is no mountain, then there is." Usually, as we go about our day, we are focused on what we think of as external phenomena: When will the rain stop? How can I get this project done? When will my son start doing his homework? When will my political views prevail? And on and on. Our days are swept away by streams of thought about these outer forms, these mountains. Ultimately this book is about realizing mindful, engaged intimacy with all these mountains: our loved ones, environment, family, work, politics. However, first we will follow the age-old practice of focusing inward, of not seeing the mountains but seeing our own inner landscape. This will open up a new, fresh, deeper engagement with the vast and amazing mountain always right before us.

If we're going to start with the self, I suppose we ought to have a sense of what "self" means. To be honest, I'm not exactly sure. I can tell you that right now it seems to me that I am here, a self, calmly engaged in the act of typing, listening to a breeze carry a light rain through the mulberry trees outside my open window. It feels distinctly like I (a self) am observing sounds and doing things. Do you have a sense of being a self doing and experiencing things right now?

Things get a little trickier as I investigate further. It seems to me that I am typing, but if I think about it differently I might say that my hands are moving across the keys of this laptop. So are these hands mine or are they me? Am I typing or are my hands doing it? I feel quite calm, but you might say also that I *am* calm. So is calm myself or something that I feel?

Have you ever found yourself saying, "I am so angry"? Boy, I have. It feels quite different to say "I feel anger." Is the anger you, or is it something you are experiencing? Of course, generally, rather than saying any of those things, we just think bad thoughts about some supposedly external thing, "Where'd you get your driver's license, moron? A Cracker Jack box?!" Noticing our feeling and taking our attention off the external form is a good step, and that opens the door for studying the self.

Mindfully investigating aspects of what we usually consider to be our "self" is central to the original teachings on mindfulness from early Buddhism. It is fundamental to these practices' capacity to promote well-being. In the *Four Foundations of Mindfulness Sutra*, most of the practices focus on mindfulness of our body, feelings, and mental states. We take something that we might generally think of as ourselves and make it the object of our mindfulness. If we experience anger, rather than thinking and believing "I am angry," we mindfully see anger. We develop the ability to see things we thought of as self—as I, me, or mine—as just phenomena that are occurring. This is very powerful in helping us be free of the impulsive tendencies that are driven by emotions and the repetitive streams of thought that run through our minds. Wouldn't it be great if, when the thought goes through your mind, "I'm terrible at this, I'll never get it done," rather than believing it's true and giving up, you could just notice that a thought has occurred, like a few drops of rain on the window, and go back to doing what you really want to do?

Mindfulness enables us to bring many aspects of ourselves into conscious awareness so that we don't have to be driven by them. Tension, pleasure, lassitude, excitement, anxiety, and pain all dwell in the body and impel our behavior. Emotions and thoughts zoom by, unexamined, and we wander through our lives unaware of their enormous driving power. It doesn't have to be that way. Freedom is an option. Carl Jung wrote, "Until you make the unconscious conscious, it will direct your life and you will call it fate." A great deal of the power of mindfulness is in the fact that it allows us to bring unconscious aspects of self into the light of awareness.

However, mindfulness of self goes deeper and opens up a path to a vast, mysterious intimacy. Intimacy in this practice begins with ourselves. When we focus awareness just on how our body is, just on our emotional state, we will begin to feel more intimate with ourselves. You can't have intimacy without paying attention. A recent study on marriages showed that one of the most effective indicators for whether marriages were healthy and would last was how often couples really paused to pay attention to each other. Intimacy begins with a feeling of connection. When you stop to pay attention to how your body and mind are, you will find a little closeness with yourself. It may feel good, and it may feel bad. A lot of us have walls against intimacy with ourselves. But if we commit to the mindfulness practices focused on elements of the self that will be laid out in the next three chapters, intimacy will slowly flower.

Humans inherently experience a sense of alienation from the world. We believe the world is out there apart from us, and time is passing by; the things we love break or fall away, lovers leave, friends move, parents die. It's painful. The path of intimacy can allow us to step through the veil of alienation into connection. But the path starts with intimacy with ourselves, for perhaps saddest of all, we are alienated from ourselves. We move through life unaware of our feelings, of our deepest callings, of the ever-present and ever-changing sensations of being in a human form. Let us commit together to find intimacy with who we are. If we do this we can become attuned to what truly matters to us. Rather than enacting unconscious habits, we can find an empowered life based on our true heart, or what Dainin Katagiri called "our inmost request."

As a Zen teacher I have gotten pretty friendly with paradox, and mindfulness of self opens up a doozy. The original teachings on mindfulness, which emphasize a lot of what I've gone through so far, ultimately have a surprising aim. They are designed to help us realize that there is nothing we can find that is our self. As one goes through the various mindfulness practices, one sees that absolutely everything that can be brought into the light of mindful awareness is just an occurrence, a momentary phenomenon, not a lasting self. A friend of mine was cleaning his house with his wife and thought, "I should clear some of this big stack of books off the end table by my bed." Well, he started cleaning up and the next thing you know he said, "Wow, there's no end table here, it's just a bunch of books!" His wife said dryly, "I know." This is kind of like Buddha hearing from one of his students after they'd practiced mindfulness of self—of body, feelings, and mind—for a good long time; sometimes they realized there was no central lasting quality, just fleeting phenomena. I can imagine the Buddha's gentle smile and "I know." This idea of seeing through the self may be very familiar or seem utterly bizarre, but the key thing is that throughout

Buddhist and other spiritual literature from all over the world, people have reported seeing through the self and expressed this as a vast, ineffable intimacy with everything. They have also tended to lead lives of joy, love, and compassion.

We don't know whether you or I will be seeing through ourselves completely or not, but the possibility of shedding our sense of alienation and opening up to connection is so worth working for. Parents do it with their children every day, and if they didn't there would be no human race. Friends do it, and they bear their companions through great suffering. People who care about their environment do it by choosing to take the bus or ride a bike to work instead of drive, and Martin Luther King Jr. did it when he sat in a Birmingham jail and wrote, "I cannot sit idly by in Atlanta and not be concerned about what happens in Birmingham . . . We are caught in an inescapable network of mutuality." I invite you to dive into the practices in the next few chapters. These practices of cultivating mindfulness of body, emotion, and mind can help you become intimate with yourself, be free from harmful habits, live from the bottom of your heart, and realize your intimacy with everyone and everything.

4. Body

Mindfulness of body is the first of the four foundations of mindfulness taught in early Buddhist literature. It is the foundation of the foundation. Many other teachings show that all aspects of the Buddhist path to liberation from suffering can be realized through mindfulness of body. When I started meditation practice I was also working with a mental health therapist who focused on awareness of body, and I recall how astonishing, simple, immediate, and transformative it was to know the body, right here. It's still pretty wondrous, just feeling my back sinking into this chair right now as my eyes subtly move to follow these words I type.

In the *Four Foundations of Mindfulness Sutra*, the mindfulness of body practices fall into two broad categories: awareness of bodily sensations and visualizations of the body's impermanence.

At Minnesota Zen Meditation Center, where I have been practicing and teaching for years, our main meditation practice falls into the former category: sitting in an upright posture and being aware of breathing.

We allow this practice to dissolve into objectless meditation sometimes, and we do various other types of meditation now and again, but basically the main practice is awareness of bodily sensations. We can cultivate and carry mindfulness of body in any situation, but without some sitting practice to cultivate it, it is very difficult to maintain and develop. Although we may experience deep mindfulness of body in activities like dance, basketball, yoga, cooking, or carpentry, they are unlikely to provide a solid foundation for development of the other aspects of mindfulness and intimacy to which this book is an invitation.

Practice: Mindfulness of Breath

Find a position where you can sit upright with a stable lower body. Invite the whole body to relax around that stability and the strength of the spine. By practicing meditation in an upright posture we feel our own energy; we embody our nobility and agency in the world. This provides a safe space to feel ease. Sitting still and focusing on breathing can be very relaxing, so our upright posture helps us to balance alertness with calm; it keeps us from falling asleep. The point is not to look some certain way or to have a correct or good posture, but rather to find your own energy for being upright and to put your attention into your body.

Having established an upright posture, focus on breathing. Although there are many wonderful yogic practices that involve controlling breathing, mindfulness just focuses on awareness of the sensations of breathing without any attempt at control. We don't have to think about, judge, analyze, or anticipate breathing. Just feel what it's like.

Choose some particular area of the body to notice the breathing: in the nostrils, at the back of the throat, or in the abdomen. The early teachings on this practice consistently refer to mindfulness of breath *in* the breath, so although we have chosen a specific object to focus on, try to move toward intimacy with this object, not coolly observing it from afar, but settling awareness directly in the felt sensations of air moving into the body and out, of the body expanding and contracting with the flow. The breath does not know how to imagine the future or ruminate about the past. If we rest our attention on the breath, our attention will naturally reside in the present moment.

Don't worry if thoughts tend to sweep you away from awareness of the breath and the posture. This is common; we sit down to practice mindfulness of breath and body, to meditate, and within seconds we are absorbed in a stream of thought. We realize we're swept away and we notice our breathing, but again we are swept away. This is okay; this is normal. Just being aware of and intimate with this process is good.

The kind of awareness we are cultivating is compassionate and curious. Every breath is unique, and every breath matters. This compassion doesn't have to fix or control anything. It is pure presence. This curiosity is not trying to analyze or figure things out; it's just really open to seeing what's here. If we find that as we practice mindfulness of breath we have an impulse to control, fix, or judge the breath, that is OK; we simply return to just being mindful of the breath *in* the breath, just settling awareness in the sensations, with nothing extra. If this doesn't seem to be happening, that is OK too; just see how this breath is right now. Just cultivate intimacy with the breath. You are already intimate with the breath; you are totally mutually dependent. It is always there to support you.

Mindfulness of breathing often has a calming effect. It is rhythmic; it is simple. When we focus on what's right here we can let go of all the rumination and imagination about the past and future and rest in what is. However, anything may arise during this practice: all kinds of thoughts and any kind of feeling you can imagine. If this happens, you're not doing it wrong. Just return to this breath. Come home to the body.

I have been describing formal sitting meditation practice, but at any time during the day you can just pause and take three mindful breaths. I encourage you to do this frequently and see what happens.

———————

For many people, practicing this simple approach to sitting meditation is difficult. Over the years I have met hundreds, probably thousands, of people who would like to practice meditation in this way but don't. They report that they feel much better when they do the practice and that it reflects their deepest values, but they just don't take the time. I cannot recommend enough that you find support within yourself and from other people for practicing sitting meditation focused on mindfulness of breath. Books can help, listening to your heart is key, and if there is any way to find other people to sit with, or to find a teacher whom you find encouraging, such support can be great for your own aspiration. Make specific plans to meditate, but be kind to yourself when you don't follow through. Don't give up.

We can bring mindfulness of body into every aspect of our days, just noticing what the sensations of the body are as we walk, sit, stand, or lie down. Feeling the sensations of water on the skin as we stand in the shower, feeling warmth on our face as we turn to the sun, noticing the ache in our back as we stand up from a long stressful day, feeling the rough then smooth surface of a carrot as we peel, or feeling the warmth of a lover's hand as we walk hand in hand. We will dive further into these daily-life practices of mindfulness of body in the chapters on the heart, the senses, nature, romance and sex, and work and play.

The *Four Foundations of Mindfulness Sutra* takes a surprising turn halfway through the section on the first foundation, mindfulness of body. We start with mindfulness of breath, posture, and the bodily sensations of daily activities, but then we move to mindfulness of the unattractiveness of the body and visualization of the body's decomposition after death. These last two are not at the forefront of the mindfulness movement that's sweeping the nation these days. They are challenging. The first involves visualizing all the parts of the body that we usually ignore—the organs, the body fluids, the waste we have not yet expelled. The second involves either going to a charnel ground, essentially an aboveground cemetery, or imagining being in one and seeing the process of the human body rotting. First we are instructed to become intimate with the experience of bodily sensation, then we imagine it being nasty and impermanent. Like many Western teachers, I am not going to emphasize these practices. However, they do have value. They point to the fact that as we become mindful of things, as we become intimate with them, we should actively acknowledge that there are things about them that are difficult, and that they will pass. This active acknowledgment should be done mindfully. This isn't about ruminating on our health problems, or habitually worrying about death and decay. It's about stopping to open up our hearts and minds with full attention, consciously and deliberately, to difficult truths.

Mindfulness, in particular mindfulness of body sensations, has a potential pitfall that mindfulness of the body's unattractiveness and impermanence is designed to counteract. For many people, being deeply attuned to bodily sensations feels great. When the body is healthy and stable, it can be wonderful to really experience our limbs as we stroll in the sun or the smooth calm of the breath moving deep in the belly. This is not to mention how wondrous eating can be if we are attuned to that simple act. I was dumbfounded when I first started doing meditation retreats and realized how amazing just putting one spoon of warm soup in my mouth could be. It's by no means bad that mindfulness of body can be so pleasant. However, if it just makes us want to hold on to our bodily pleasures, it's probably not so good. If our practice becomes about getting something momentarily pleasant for ourselves, it just contributes to the fundamental problem of human experience: our alienation and self-centered focus on getting our way. Mindfulness of the body's impermanence, of the fact that all these pleasant states will eventually go away, can remind us that life can be about something much bigger than getting nice things for ourselves right now. It can remind us of the joy and value of life based on an understanding of our intimacy with everything, with what will be here long after we are gone. Later in this book we will have time to work with this material in the chapter on dying.

If we practice mindfulness of body, we may develop a sense that our minds observe our bodies. The instruction throughout the *Four Foundations of Mindfulness Sutra* to practice mindfulness of the body *in* the body can help to counter this view and help us deeply experience bodily sensation itself without mental mediation. The idea that mind and body are separate is only that—an idea. The two are intimate. In the West we are inculcated with a strong sense that the mind rules the body. Conversely, neuroscientists and psychologists are now pointing out how physical processes in the body govern thought, emotion, and behavior. I have noticed that when my thoughts are racing, my breath tends to be shallow, and my shoulders tense. Who is in charge here?

As we develop mindfulness of the body it's good to notice all the sensations, whether we like them or not. Most of the sensations in the body are very subtle. When we bring the attention to the breath, perhaps noticing the abdomen expand and contract, it's easy to see why we often ignore it. It's not sending us any loud messages. Sometimes, however, we have discomfort, intense pain, or deep pleasure. If pain is intense it's best to do something that might help us feel better, but mindfulness practice invites us to see many of these states just as they are, without trying to avoid or control them. If you are practicing upright sitting and mindfulness of breath and you feel a little discomfort in your leg, see if you can be aware of the feeling without focusing on it. Let the mindfulness of the body be broad, including both the subtle and strong sensations. You may notice that sometimes breath is shallow and ragged, at other times deep and slow. You may notice tension in the back that you usually ignore. All these sensations, no matter how subtle or intense, are deeply connected to how your mind and emotions work. If your back is tense, whether you notice it or not, it will tend to create tense thoughts and feelings. However, if you deeply know your back is tense and are mindful of the breath, you may be able to take a brief break from tense thoughts, and you will create the habit of having a subtle break between the loop of tense body, tense feeling, and tense thoughts. This process is not done by controlling things but through compassionate, nonjudgmental awareness—mindfulness—of the body.

So do feelings produce bodily states or vice versa? Does my mind make me tense or does the tension in my body make me have all these crazy repetitive thoughts? If I'm deeply mindful of my body, what exactly is my mind? Mindfulness opens up as many questions as it provides answers, and intimacy is not about figuring out or controlling. Intimacy knows that body and mind are different—we experience that to be true—but it also knows they are completely interdependent, they are one and the same. When we take care of one we take care of all. The basis for this taking care is compassionate, nonjudgmental awareness.

5. Mind

Yesterday, about ten minutes into guiding a meditation, I said, "As I have been talking and inviting you to attend to your posture and breath, your mind has probably swept you away a few times. Maybe right now you're so absorbed in thought, you barely even know I'm talking." A laughing voice in the back of the room said, "Stop reading my mind!" We all had a chuckle and settled into the sensations of laughing bodies. I'm no mind reader, but I know how good it is to make friends with the fact that in meditation many thoughts will come and go.

The human mind is conditioned to generate thought. Over thousands of years, natural selection developed our big brains and capacity for language-based thinking. For most people, becoming aware of the relentlessness of the mind's generation of thoughts is one of the most startling aspects of mindfulness practice. We think we'll simply sit down and clear our minds, but instead we just become very aware that our mind keeps telling us stories—and that we are so thoroughly mesmerized by these stories that we constantly lose awareness of our breath and our posture. Although we may not be getting what we wanted, we're getting something very good: awareness of mind.

Mindfulness of breath and posture naturally serve to generate mindfulness of mind. Even the smallest break in thinking gives us the chance to notice that the mind is telling us stories. Instead of just listening to the mind's stories as if they were ironclad facts, we become aware that thinking is part of the phenomena of the present moment. Thoughts are just something that happens.

Seeing that thoughts are just phenomena, like clouds passing in the sky or the sound of a plane passing overhead, diminishes the dangerous aspects of their power. Thoughts are powerful, and that's good. If you have the thought "I want to honor everyone's opinions and feelings at this meeting and do my best to collaborate for the greatest good with everyone there," that is good; it can help you be open-minded, brave, and kind. However, on many occasions our thoughts are not very helpful, and their power is such that sometimes they can be disastrous. For instance, thoughts that people of different religions, nations, and races are subhuman, evil, or inferior have contributed to massive atrocities. On a smaller scale, every day unexamined thoughts profoundly limit what we choose to do, our happiness, and how much we contribute to the world.

If we realize that our thoughts are just phenomena, it opens the door for acting from a deeper and more intentional aspect of ourselves. We free ourselves from being driven by unconscious habits of thought.

Because awareness that mind is generating thoughts tends to arise naturally from the practice of mindfulness of body, we don't necessarily need to practice mindfulness of mind separately. In the *Four Foundations of Mindfulness Sutra*, mindfulness of mind is the third foundation, but in this book I will include that type of practice in the next chapter on mindfulness of emotion; most of the things the sutra describes there are emotional. For now, I just encourage you not to let meditation and mindfulness practice become a fight with the mind. Your mind will keep generating thought, and you will forget what you are trying to be mindful of and become completely absorbed in streams of thought. It's part of the deal. When you notice you are absorbed in thought, it's not a problem; in that very moment, just bring the attention back to the object of mindfulness— breath or posture perhaps. Do this with resolve, but also do it with compassion. Activist Audre Lorde once wrote, "The quality of light by which we scrutinize our lives has direct bearing upon the product which we live, and upon the changes which we hope to bring about through those lives."

Mindfulness practice is often understood as a means of training the mind. By sitting down over and over again and practicing mindfulness of breath, the mind becomes conditioned to be aware of breath, to be aware of thinking as it arises, to let go of thoughts, and to see thoughts as just one of the many things that are happening. If we train the mind in this way we will find that thoughts are no longer so dominant, and our experience is one in which our sense of our body and the other five senses is more balanced with the mind's gyrations. This is training not by controlling thoughts but by returning attention to the breath. It is a gentle, kind way of training. To work, it must be done on a regular basis for a sustained period of time. I'm hoping to do it every day for the rest of my life, because I've seen how liberating it has been to do it for the last fifteen years.

It's nice to compare training the mind with mindfulness to training a puppy. Training a puppy is good. A well-trained dog can get along with other dogs and be a wonderful friend to human beings. But wild dogs are amazing too. African wild dogs and wolves all over the world have an amazing and beautiful way of being that doesn't need human interference.

Mindfulness teachings tend to use the language of training, but Mahayana teachings on intimacy often encourage us to let things be wild, let them be free. Zen Master Shitou was asked about practice and enlightenment. He said, "The blue sky does not obstruct the white cloud's flight." A blue-sky mind has room for everything to come and go.

There is no separate kind of practice I can offer called "intimacy with mind." We are all already intimate with it. Even so, you can find a vast, spacious blue-sky mind where thoughts float by like clouds, unimpeded. In intimacy we don't have to wait for the mind to be trained to act the way we want. We don't have to make wolves do anything at all. We can just offer ourselves to how things are in this moment, in this world, and make room for things to be as they are. The part of the mind that wants to control things and arrange them to our tastes can float by in the sky, and the sky can embrace everything and let it go.

6. Heart

Have you ever seen someone laughing in the rain? Or someone stoop-shouldered, shuffling along on a green and sunny day? Perhaps in a time of crisis you've seen someone respond with resolve and energy, and someone else collapse into fear or despair. Maybe someone you know gets testy and then you know it's best to leave them alone. When a loved one is dying, sometimes people are overwhelmed with pain and can barely take care of their basic needs, and sometimes they leap into frantic action to avoid their feelings, and at other times they only know one thing: profound, all-encompassing acceptance and love. I've seen all this in others and in myself as well.

One of the clearest insights of my years of meditation is how powerfully my emotions color my experience, my perception of the world. When I am angry, I feel isolated, and I feel the need to control, the need for swift action. When sad, I feel alone and like there's nothing worth doing; I feel like staying in bed. When I'm afraid, I feel vulnerable, like I have to get away.

When I am ashamed, I feel abandoned, like everything is pointless, and like I am fundamentally flawed. When I feel intimacy with people and my environment, on the other hand, I feel connected, I trust what's happening, and I am patient and engaged.

Afflictive emotions are the reason the practice of mindfulness exists, and why the kind of intimacy this book is about arose as central to Buddhist thought. Buddhism is at its root a set of practices and ideas designed to free human beings from afflictive emotion. The four noble truths are known as the first and most central teaching of Buddhism, and essentially say this: you can alleviate suffering through ethical living and meditation. The ethics of this tradition are based in intimacy, on understanding our interdependence with all things. The basic practice of meditation is mindfulness.

We can alleviate suffering through mindfulness and intimacy with all kinds of things: our bodies, our minds, our families, our habits of consumption, the people who bother us. The list is long, and we'll explore many of these in this book. However, mindfulness of emotions is central to transforming our lives—and hence the world, with which we are always already intimately connected.

The power of mindfulness of emotion is best explained using some Buddhist concepts, particularly those of the great teacher Vasubandhu, of the Yogacara school. Basically, this school says that any intentional, cognitive, or emotional impulse plants a seed in our unconscious. That seed will bear similar fruit at some later date; we don't know when. For instance, when we are babies, we hear the sound "mom" many times, and it always points back to the same person. Seeds of cognition are planted, and we associate the sound "mom" with our mother. In the future, when we see her, those seeds bear fruit and we think, "Mom!" So words and thoughts form patterns in our minds. The same thing happens with emotions. When we have a feeling, it plants a seed, and later we will experience a similar feeling again. All the times you felt irritated waiting in line plant seeds, so that the next time you are in a line, you are more likely to be irritated. All the times you felt calm and safe at home plant seeds, so you will again feel calm and safe at home. The Buddha's great insight about this process was that if you are mindful of any harmful fruit that is arising right now, its power will be exhausted and it will not plant another similar seed.

Even the best of us are generally not very mindful of our feelings. We are absorbed in thought, believing the stories and perceptions of the world our feelings create. For example, when angry, rather than being deeply aware of what it is like to experience anger, we just think about how someone else is wrong. When we are worried, rather than knowing the hard-beating heart, the butterflies in our stomach, and the feeling of fear itself, we are just absorbed in a long line of thoughts about dreadful outcomes. Mindfulness of emotions requires deeply experiencing our feelings and letting go of our mind's focus on its stream of thinking. Let's say you are anxious about a conversation you need to have with one of your parents. If you can pause from worrying and focus your attention on how you feel, you directly see the feeling, and the fruits of past worries that are manifesting melt away in the light of mindfulness, without planting new seeds. The seeds you are planting in this moment are seeds of mindfulness, which will bear fruit someday. You create a mind that is less likely to be anxious and more likely to be mindful.

Mindfulness of emotions can be developed and practiced in many ways, with varying degrees of subtlety and focus. Sitting down with someone to talk about how you feel is a good way to begin to be aware of emotions. This has been a key part of many modern psychological methods, and it is a great way to develop intimacy with friends. However, as long as we are focused on words and describing them, we are still not getting right to the heart of the matter. In a conversation like this it really helps to pause, let go of all the thinking, and direct attention toward the feeling itself. This can be hard to do. It's good to practice in meditation to build our ability.

Practice: Mindfulness of Emotions

To practice mindfulness of emotions formally in meditation it's best to find a stable upright posture, as I would recommend for all meditation practice.

Because the mind is so conditioned to dominate our experience and try to resolve our emotional difficulties with a bunch of planning, it is difficult to hold awareness on emotions. It's best to start with mindfulness of breath (see chapter 4), which works well as a starting point for just about any kind of meditation practice.

As you find a few breaks in the relentless stream of thought, as you find a little time in which awareness rests in the breath, you can begin to direct attention to how you feel: relaxed, angry, fidgety, joyous, anxious, tired, whatever it is. Feelings often come in chords rather than single notes. This isn't about naming or nailing them down. It's about just being aware of them as they are. It may seem difficult, because there is not a place where feelings live; although they do relate closely to bodily sensations, you can't find your feelings in a place. Just see if you can know how you are emotionally right now. Sometimes the relationship to the body can help. If you notice the breath is shallow and tight as you are breathing, for example, it may help you to be aware of irritation or anxiety.

Sometimes there may be almost no feelings you can find. That's just fine. At other times they may be strong, and you will find that awareness of them causes the mind to leap into action: "I've got this!" The thinking mind seems to think it's the answer to everything. See if you can be aware of the process as it unfolds. If emotions are so intense that you can't hold any awareness on them, it might be best to go back to the breath. If they are so strong that they are almost unbearable, the breath is a good refuge, and I really recommend you find a meditation teacher to provide you some support.

Here's a brief, simple, and effective way to practice mindfulness of emotions. Several times a day, stop what you are doing, take three mindful breaths, and then focus on how you feel for a few seconds. This will plant seeds of mindfulness, diminish the power of afflictive emotional habits, and cultivate awareness of how your emotions affect your life. You will begin to notice how the feelings of which you are mindful relate to other aspects of your experience and your actions.

Here's one more related practice: actively cultivating beneficial emotions. Recent science shows that sustaining attention on pleasant mental states for a little longer than we usually would conditions the mind to experience those mental states again. In Buddhist terms, it plants beneficial seeds. As you go through your day, try and actively notice when you feel good: when you feel happy, calm, energetic, etc. When you notice you feel this way, pause and focus on

the feeling and your sensations in the present moment—
the body, sights, sounds, smells, and tastes. Try and hold
this attention for thirty seconds. Plant some seeds of wellness, and move on.

———————————

Sometimes in Zen we encourage finding "no gap"
between ourselves and what is happening: total intimacy. We may settle into the breath so deeply that
there is not an "I" observing breathing—there is simply breath. We may sometimes find this kind of total
immersion in experience outside of meditation as well:
in arts or in experiences where we are deeply connected
to another, in acts of love. Some kinds of mindfulness
training have this flavor. The *Four Foundations of Mindfulness Sutra* encourages "mindfulness of the body, in the
body." No gap. However, when we first start practicing
mindfulness of emotions and when our emotions are
very powerful, it's probably best to practice with a gap.
We want to make our awareness big and focused on
seeing the feeling without becoming overwhelmed or
absorbed by it. Mindfulness has the flavor of cool, calm
observation, and we can bring this to our feelings to
help them be seen, exhaust the power of their seeds,
and cool off when they are hot.

If our practice becomes very stable, usually after
years of regular meditation, we may be able to move
toward total intimacy with strong emotions, with no

gap. To sit still and upright in great anger as we breathe in and out and the light of a candle flickers on the wall takes courage and strength of practice, but it can open us up to a well of strength and acceptance that is oceanic. Shunryu Suzuki said, "Let anger be a great bonfire that burns itself away."

When we are with others it's good to be mindful of emotions, and we'll discuss this more later in the book. If we start by focusing our awareness on how people feel, we're able to feel more connected, more intimate. It's important to develop the ability to discern when it's good to be mindful of other people's emotions, with a cool, calm observation, and when we can be more intimate, when we can really join a person in their feeling. Generally the test is whether your attention to the other person's emotions are triggering your own.

Last year I was at a Black Lives Matter occupation after a police officer killed a young, beloved man named Philando Castile. Organizers were giving speeches through a megaphone, and on the margins people were milling around and chatting. I was practicing meditation. Suddenly, near me, a man started shouting obscenities and violent intentions into a television camera. I felt my heart tighten and recoil and my mind began to proliferate judgments, so I took a moment to be mindful of my emotional reaction. As my reactivity settled, I was able to hear him with mindfulness, to just observe. Then I was able to open up and let in the raw rage and anguish of his message, that he felt brutalized and oppressed by the people who claimed to protect him. Because I took a moment to observe my own reactions, I was able to actually hear him.

7. Dying

The psychologist Elisabeth Kübler-Ross transformed American culture by encouraging us to give up being a "death-denying society." She helped many of us to see that death is an integral part of life and a process with room for tremendous transformation and healing. Her mindfulness of death has had an immense impact on how people are treated and live their final days, and how people are supported who are losing loved ones. To acknowledge and call to mind death as a part of life is a basic way to practice mindfulness of death, but not surprisingly this is not the most popular mindfulness practice around. Death is scary, and death is painful. Death is often taboo. And so we shy away, though Kübler-Ross helped show us a way of courage.

Buddhist mindfulness teachings also return frequently to mindfulness of death. In the *Four Foundations of Mindfulness Sutra*, the first foundation is mindfulness of body, and about half of the practices in that first section deal with mindfulness of death. They involve either actually going to an aboveground cemetery (common in India twenty-five hundred years ago) to mindfully observe bodies decomposing or visualizing the same in meditation. I will not describe these particular techniques here, but it's clear that in the original understanding of how mindfulness works, focusing awareness on and fully acknowledging death was key to finding liberation from suffering.

Reminders of the inevitability of death run throughout many cultures. Since the time of ancient Rome, the *memento mori* (reminder of death) has been a common artistic theme. Countless European oil paintings have a skull somewhere gazing out at us through blank and empty eye sockets. A quick internet search will yield hundreds of deities from cultures all over the world associated with death. These archetypes remind us of the tremendous, inevitable power of change and loss.

Mindfulness of death helps us to be strong and brave in the face of life's greatest difficulties. When I was in middle school one of my cousins died at my house of a congenital illness. Later, I was embarrassed to talk about him, but my mother encouraged me and made space for me to speak. At the time, I did not know that she was studying Kübler-Ross, preparing to volunteer at a hospice, and developing artwork focused on impermanence. Years later my father was diagnosed, fairly young, with terminal cancer. My mother, who had been married to him for forty years, took care of him and her own grieving with grace and an open heart. We wept a great deal together as light streamed in the hospital windows and his life drained away. But we also smiled and loved with all our hearts. Although she did no traditional mindfulness practices, her years of acknowledging and facing death enabled her to show great courage and poise in the face of loss. Her example opened up the door for me to grow rather than wilt in the face of grief.

Mindfulness of death helps us to recall the preciousness of each moment. It is so easy for us to go through life consumed by trivial concerns. When a loved one is dying most of us see in stark relief how things that once consumed our minds and hearts are actually small and insignificant. In my twenties, when I was addicted to alcohol and drugs, it was largely the awareness of death following the losses of my father and grandparents that brought me to Zen practice and to recovery. Their deaths allowed me to see the possibility of a life of meaning, above the waves of the ocean of exhausting and petty concerns in which I almost drowned.

All things pass. A great deal of the suffering and dissatisfaction we experience comes from our reaction to the fact that what we want to hold on to goes away. Lives end, bike tires go flat, beach vacations end and we find ourselves standing in a snowbank waiting for the bus, children with whom we laughed yesterday slam doors and storm away today, our moods shift, our favorite season fades away. The world will unfold in its own way, not according to our preferences. Mindfulness of death allows us to learn that we can remain calm, engaged, and even joyful for this unfolding, even in the most trying of times.

By cultivating mindfulness of death, we can prepare ourselves to meet death with courage, and this opens the door for profound intimacy. Being with their dying can be one of the most intimate experiences we ever have with loved ones. I am profoundly grateful I received encouragement and support for spending lots of time with my father as he died. Some of our most intimate moments came during his last years of life, when he was racked by illness and his life was fading. We found time to speak to each other from the heart, and we found time to heal wounds from our past errors. The last word he ever spoke was *love*.

Practice: The Five Remembrances

Here is a simple Buddhist practice that takes less than one minute per day for cultivating mindfulness of death and transience: reciting the five remembrances. Once a day, stop whatever else you are doing, take three mindful breaths, and recite the verse below. As you recite it focus on two things: the words and how you feel. Practice being present to your emotional state as you recall death and impermanence. When you are done reciting feel free to let it all go; there's no need to dwell on the issue. However, if emotions are triggered please return to compassionate, nonjudgmental awareness of how you feel. Don't repress what arises.

> I am of the nature to age; I cannot avoid aging.
> I am of the nature to become ill; I cannot avoid illness.
> I am of the nature to die; I cannot avoid death.
> I will be parted from all that is dear and beloved to me.
> Actions are my possessions, actions are my protection, actions are the ground on which I stand, actions are the womb from which I have sprung. As I do so shall I become.

The first four are reminders of transience; the last is a message of empowerment. The first four recall that life is fleeting, that things we don't want will happen no matter what. The last encourages us to focus on this moment of action, on what we do now. Since everything changes, this very moment is our greatest opportunity. In the words of the physicist Neil deGrasse Tyson, "It is the knowledge that I'm going to die that creates the focus that I bring to being alive, the urgency of accomplishment, the need to express love, now, not later."

Though we cannot stave off aging, illness, and loss, we can always contribute something in this very moment. Though death will come, you are alive right now, so you can do some beneficial action. Being mindful is an excellent and beneficial act. Acts of generosity, of courage, of kindness all contribute to the greatest good. You have an amazing opportunity as long as you are alive.

8. Values and Meaning

How often are you living for what matters to you most? Think of those times when life seemed most meaningful and valuable to you. Compare this to the times in your life where you were consumed with some concern that seemed unimportant years later, or just days or hours later. The opportunity to jump joyfully into a life of meaning is always right here, but the chatter of the human mind so frequently turns life into a wash of petty concerns. "Am I going to be five minutes late?" "Why did she say that to me?" "Why is this app downloading so slowly?"

Being mindful and intimate with our values can help us find a more meaningful life. If our values are supported by mindfulness and intimacy, then remembering these values can give us energy to practice.

When I say *values* I mean foundational ideas like *love, peace, compassion, kindness, harmony, intimacy, freedom, justice, honesty, courage.* (It's best to keep these in broad, powerful words without spending a lot of time on semantics.) Maybe some of these don't reflect your values. That is A-OK. It's good for us to encourage each other to continually refine our values, and as a Zen teacher part of my job is to help people with that process. However, at the very bottom, your values are your own to realize. At root, the power of values has to come from each individual heart.

_____

Practice: Mindfulness of Values

It's good to cultivate mindfulness of our values alone, with friends, and in community. If this seems foreign to you I encourage you to try doing it alone first.

Cultivating values alone: Sit down a few times with a pen and paper and write down things that you value. Keep it simple. This should not be cognitively driven but should come from the heart. At the end it's good to make a list of one to ten words that are simple and reflect what you actually believe and feel. Put the list somewhere you will see it daily and read through it, or remember the words and repeat them to yourself. This can help you to become more intimate with what really matters to you. Maybe the next time you are about to do something harmful—like say something nasty to someone else, or to yourself—you will remember these values and choose another way.

Cultivating values with friends and family: Joking around with loved ones and talking about all kinds of little things is fun, but I really encourage you to find the time and the courage to talk to these folks about what really matters to you, as well. This can be scary for some of us, and not everyone will want to join you, but give it a shot. Try not to judge or become defensive if people don't meet you halfway. This isn't about controlling people. If you open the door to talking about life on the level of your deepest values, you open the door for a much deeper intimacy with the people in your life.

Cultivating values in community: I cannot recommend enough finding a community or communities of people that support and encourage you to live from your values. It's also good if they help you develop and grow, and challenge you if you are stuck. Spiritual communities, social justice groups, addiction recovery groups, volunteer groups . . . there are lots of options. Humans are social animals and community is powerful. I have met hundreds of people who come to the Zen center where I teach saying they have wanted to meditate for years but never do. For many of them, sitting down with the group at the Zen center and hearing teachings about the value of mindfulness is a key ingredient to a sustained meditation practice.

Cultivating values with the whole world: We have so much to learn from each other. There are so many cultures and individuals on this planet, so many species and individual animals, such a vast community of trees, grasses, pebbles, waves, and wandering beings. To begin to learn we first must listen, we must be aware. Watch the intricate coexistence of the myriad plants and birds on a lakeshore.

What can it show you about living in harmony with difference? Open up to other voices, the words of people from communities far different from your own. Especially listen to the voices of those who are pushed into the margins, those whose power is stifled, those whose values you may not otherwise ever know, those whose messages you must work to hear. Listen, seek to understand. And then let your understanding transform your values in a way that's true to you.

_____

The power of community and values has a downside. Groups of people over and over again have become convinced that some basic value is of utmost importance—that one country is better than another, that one race or religion is superior, that the most important thing is getting more money—and they have thereby caused great harm. Of course, individuals can also become too absorbed in an obsession with their values and do great harm as well. I recommend using these mindfulness practices to regularly reexamine your values in light of your own heart, your connection to your loved ones, the communities you choose to be a part of, and the whole vast community of the world. This will aerate your values so they do not harden into dogmatism.

Values are powerful. When they promote harmony they are wonderful; when they are divisive they are dangerous. This is why the deepest value I hold is intimacy: realizing interdependence. It's easy to see how intimacy promotes a lot of things most people value. Love and kindness come right to mind. But how about honesty? We're less likely to lie if we don't feel separate from someone. I value courage, and the greatest courage is often motivated by the impulse to protect people we know are a part of us—thus, people from all over the country came to stand with Southerners during the civil rights movement. There is no justice where one person or group is cut off from another, where intimacy is forgotten.

Through mindfulness of our values we can become more intimate with them and with all those around us. We can let them transform and change as we learn and see new ways to be in the world. If we keep turning toward them we can see how the small concerns that fill our days with aggravation can fade in the light of a life of meaning.

9. Not-Knowing

Your average dog can detect smells over ten thousand times more minutely than you and I can. The visual field we perceive and think is so solid is actually comprised of a tiny fraction of the electromagnetic spectrum. Our hearing captures a narrow band of the range of vibrations around and within us. Our thoughts represent an infinitesimal drop in the ocean of human thought. We sit on a tiny stone in the middle of an incomprehensibly vast universe, with no idea of what aspects of the universe we may not even have thought to look for or imagine because they are out of the range of our five limited senses and our tiny stream of little thoughts, and we find ourselves so convinced that we are right and know what's going on.

If we really open up to our intimacy with the vastness of the universe and the vastness of what we don't know, it can be scary, it can be humbling, and it can be freeing. In the last hundred years philosophers, artists, and our great global cultural milieu all call into question beliefs that communities have held for thousands of years. We are given the opportunity to face the vast chasm of our ignorance, our not-knowing. Picture a French existentialist pondering the night sky beneath a plume of cigarette smoke, or picture a teenager at home in front of a laptop trying to figure out what life is about with the mass of competing and contradictory views flying by. It's scary to stay in not-knowing, so usually we will form an ideology and begin to trust those views that agree with ours and not trust—or even hate—other views. Our need to know can lock us in a trap. I suspect we all know someone who has gotten so locked in their fixed views that it cuts them off from other people. They may find like-minded folks, but this provides a small, closed intimacy rather than a really expansive one.

Of course, it's good to have convictions, and it's good to pursue knowledge, but it's best to leaven this by cultivating our not-knowing. Einstein and Copernicus used their knowledge but had enough not-knowing to be open to seeing something no one else could perceive. Before Susan B. Anthony or Gandhi arrived at their convictions—that the world would be better with women voting and mass nonviolent actions—they had to have enough not-knowing to imagine something profoundly new was possible. It's good to cultivate not-knowing in general, to stay loose. It's really powerful to access it when you are stuck, or you feel hatred or alienation from someone or something. Not-knowing is one of the most powerful ways to dissolve division and limitation into intimacy and freedom.

Practice: Objectless Meditation and Not-Knowing

Objectless meditation is an excellent way to cultivate our not-knowing. It is fundamentally an act of not-knowing; just sit and things are. They're not what you think they are. What are they? Just don't figure it out. Instructions for objectless meditation are often paradoxical because paradox doesn't make a place for knowledge to land. I once heard a prominent Zen teacher talking about objectless meditation, which he'd been doing for about fifty years. He said, "I don't really know what it is."

First, find a stable, upright posture.

Then, check in with your mind: if the thinking mind is busy, objectless meditation is probably not a good fit. Try another practice, like mindfulness of breath, to help settle the mind first.

If the mind is quiet, and awareness includes bodily sensation, sights, sounds, and emotions, try releasing any attempt to focus on anything in particular or make anything happen. Rest in panoramic awareness. Let go. As Kosho Uchiyama Roshi advises, "Open the hand of thought." Or as Seung Sahn taught: "Only don't know." Practice just sitting.

Here's another way to cultivate not-knowing: Pause at any time to look at something and ask, "What is this?" Then let the thinking mind rest. Don't try to figure out the answer; to ask the question is enough. You can teach yourself to not-know.

This not-knowing can be very deep. I've heard folks practicing objectless meditation on long retreats describe their sense of time or their sense of being separate from other things vanishing, of white bare walls becoming utterly unknown and wondrous images, as close as the heart, still just white. True, it sounds kind of trippy, and no, it's not magic; folks don't become perfect and get superpowers, at least as far as I've seen. But people do find a freedom, an agility, that comes from opening up to possibility and loosening constriction. People shed the binding walls of their limited ideas and find intimacy with the dynamism of the moment.

You can bring the attitude of not-knowing to mindfulness. When breathing, you may find that breath after breath begins to look the same. If this happens, open up to not-knowing, really see each breath for what it is now, not what the thinking mind decides it is. In not-knowing there is no boredom. Everything is always fresh.

When you are in a conflict with someone, try pausing to reflect on all you don't know. Then focus on knowing what you can do to promote the greatest possible good. Rather than "knowing" what you should control in order to create some imagined outcomes, just know what to do. You can use not-knowing to let go of what's beyond your control and step into your empowerment, your moment of choice. You may not know how to get your favorite candidate elected to the presidency, but you can choose to walk to the voting booth. That big crowd of Christians in Cairo in the Arab Spring might not have known how to end religious hatred, but they could make a human wall of protection around a crowd of their praying Muslim brothers and sisters.

Keep it simple. When you are with your beloved, your family, your friends, open up to not-knowing. Let them surprise you. Really listen. Offer your attention; open your heart.

10. Teachers

Tomoe Katagiri taught me well, mostly by staying by my side and quietly pouring her energy into what we were doing together.

Tomoe-san helped bring the art of sewing Zen monk's robes from Japan to the United States, and she was my teacher in sewing the robes that symbolized my ordination. She gave me precise instruction on the technical aspects of sewing (with which I am far from adept), but to me her real teaching lay in her embodiment of patience, attention to the present moment, and quiet, warm intimacy. It was not uncommon, as we worked side by side, for us to be silent for an hour at a time to support wholehearted focus on each stitch.

After the entire robe is sewn, which took me about a year, it is carefully ironed and folded precisely, like origami. I frequently found the sewing process frustrating, but she just calmly stitched away beside me. I recall the moment when I finished the final stitch. A moment I had been waiting for! I said, "Tomoe, I finished the robe!" I was ready for a birthday cake, or maybe some fireworks. She put down her sewing and moved to stand up as she said, "I'll turn on the iron."

I don't think she was consciously "teaching" me, but she brought me right back to what was in front of me. She modeled not living for some other time when the current task, the current manifestation of life, is done. She hadn't been waiting for me to finish, and she realized nothing is ever really finished. Life goes on. All things connect. She took care of the world by focusing on the life at hand, and that was teaching enough for me.

Teachers can provide support and encouragement for you to keep cultivating mindfulness and intimacy. They can embody intimacy with things. They can provide a safe space to explore intimacy. They can model just being mindful of how you are without judgment, and they can help you find your hidden barriers and move beyond them with kindness. Teachers can also muck things up in countless ways; they are just people.

Most people who serve as teachers of the kind of mindfulness and intimacy described in this book trained in the Buddhist tradition. However, I think we will find that there are clergy from other traditions who have a deep sense of the material I'm writing about. These days many psychologists are becoming trained in this kind of work, and there are secular mindfulness-teacher-training programs popping up as well. In Zen we don't call anyone a teacher who didn't have many years of intensive training and authorization to teach from their own teacher. However, for the purposes of this book, I'd like to keep the meaning of the word *teacher* broad, so as to include people from many traditions. Generally I think to teach in this field it's good to have spent a few thousand hours meditating, studied mindfulness extensively, learned healthy boundaries, transformed one's barriers to intimacy, and practiced with various teachers.

Keeping your motivation to be mindful and cultivate intimacy can be hard. Lots of people like the idea; not that many actually sit down to meditate and do it. I think the main reason I need teachers and I teach is to keep feeding the energy of people's motivation to practice. Sure, I'll write and say lots of words and some of them will be rooted in deep and ancient wisdom from wonderful sages, but finally they are just to remind you that it's worth jumping into this moment with a willingness to let your barriers down and realize your connection to what is. I've been on retreat plenty of times, practicing meditation for hours each day, and become discouraged and exhausted: my body tired, my mind pouring out boring, repetitive stories, awareness of the moment rare and weary. Then I get up and meet with my teacher and he just says, "It's OK, here we are." He shows me how to be present by just being present to me, and his kind demeanor reminds me that intimacy is safe, that it feels good, that it is worth a lifetime of practice and commitment. I leave energized, and I sit back down to be with life on life's terms.

I love learning, so I love teachers who can convey knowledge well. I love going to a big event and seeing a teacher whose personal magnetism can bring thousands of people into a unified, connected focus. A charismatic teacher can be helpful, a knowledgeable teacher is good, but finally what I think is best is a teacher who embodies mindfulness and intimacy: someone who shows in their regular activities a sense of attention to the moment and connection to life. I don't recommend teachers who teach mindfulness with fervor and then numb their mind with drugs or alcohol. Teachers who preach interdependence and then abuse their power to have sex with students commit enormous harm; they've lost their awareness of interdependence. In order to satisfy a small need for personal intimacy, they lose awareness of vast intimacy with everything. I recommend a teacher who washes dishes with patience and attention, who meets people in conflict with a sense of connection rather than defensiveness or control, who expresses awareness of but kindness toward their own flaws and those of others.

I also don't recommend waiting to meet a teacher who is perfect, or believing that your teacher is perfect. The teacher-student relationship is between two human beings, with all the joys and challenges that intimacy entails.

Trust is key to the teacher-student relationship, and the best trust is based in the teacher's presence and connection, rather than knowledge, power, or magnetism. Trust is key because the teacher-student relationship is one of our most fertile grounds for cultivating our capacity for intimacy. Trust opens the door for intimacy, which is the path to trust. This book is about cultivating intimacy with everything. Each of us has places where we most naturally feel it. Some of us feel it most in personal conversations, others in nature, others when lost in a crowd brought together by music, others while absorbed in the characters in a book, others while cooking dinner for our loved ones. All these ways are good, but I believe that at the bottom human beings develop their capacity and strength for intimacy with other people one to one. We usually start with our mothers, or infant caregivers, long before we know any words or almost anything else. We begin to know far below the level of thought, "I am here with this person and we are absolutely interconnected." Somewhere deep in our consciousness this image of one person facing another carries enormous power. If we trust it, our capacity to build on it is strong. If we do not, the road is long. As bell hooks wrote, "Trust is the heartbeat of genuine love." Regardless of what level of trust and intimacy you had when you were very young, there will be ways in which you feel safe in intimacy and ways that you do not. Working with a teacher allows you to practice cultivating intimacy, authenticity, connection, and trust. As you become stronger in these you will find they provide a foundation for experiencing all of this with other people, with the natural world, and with yourself.

I can't recommend blind trust. No matter how wonderful your teacher is and how much you trust them, they'll make mistakes and it will hurt. Intimacy with another should always also build trust in yourself. If you have a teacher who breaks down your trust of yourself, it may be wise to reconsider the relationship. Many teachers have abused their power. It's OK to turn some power over to people, but never lose sight of your own strength, integrity, and intuition.

11. Sangha

Sangha traditionally means the community of Buddhist practitioners, but here I'd like to use the term more broadly to include any group of people who focus on cultivating mindfulness and intimacy. There are meditation and twelve-step groups, meditation groups in synagogues, contemplative prayer groups in churches, and dialectical behavior therapy groups. These all provide a community of support for the way of being this book is about. Members of marginalized communities tell me that sanghas defined around identity can be really helpful: LGBTQ, women's, or people-of-color-only meditation groups, for example. My friend and Soto teacher Bussho Lahn teaches at our Zen center, at Minnesota's Episcopal House of Prayer, and at the secular Aslan Institute, which mostly houses psychologists. The work he does with all these communities, these sanghas, is very similar, training in present-moment awareness and dissolving unhealthy barriers between ourselves and others.

In Buddhist literature we have the model of three

refuges: Buddha, Dharma, and Sangha, meaning teacher, teaching, and community of practitioners. Each of these is understood to be a place of refuge, because life can be hard. If you have a community of people to practice with, you have somewhere to go for refuge when the big stuff happens. One of our community members at our Zen center was laid off from a job she loved after twenty years. She was heartbroken, and she came and found refuge in her friends in practice (as well as her teacher and the teachings). When people lose loved ones, we pull together to provide refuge for our friends, and when depression, fear, hopelessness, and rage overtake us we have a group of people whose intimacy with us helps us feel safe in coming to them, and whose mindfulness of our suffering shows that it can be borne.

We all take refuge somewhere—in daydreaming, in shopping, in volunteering, in alcohol. Some places of refuge seem to work really well temporarily and then work really badly in the aftermath. Drugs and casual sex are often good examples of this. Television, if you pay attention, has a nice, safe quality, but does it really provide long-term benefits? Discerning what places provide a refuge that can promote mindfulness and intimacy is important. Otherwise our refuges just serve to make us numb, dependent, and isolated.

Community is excellent as a refuge because it is dynamic: we can't know what will be happening with our friends on the path. Sometimes they'll be feeling great; other times not. It helps us avoid using our refuge for numbing. Community is one of the best options for making sure our refuge doesn't keep us isolated. If I hadn't made a change in my refuges, I might have spent five hours a day reading books in my room for my whole life! Community can make us dependent, however, if it's our only refuge, so we need a balance: find your own healthy spaces outside of your practice community, find refuge in teachings and teachers, and find refuge in sitting down to meditate.

If you've spent a good deal of time with any group of people you've probably noticed that it doesn't always feel like a refuge. As the saying goes, "If you've got people, you've got problems." I've seen wonderful people who spend a great deal of time supporting others who are suffering in countless ways, but who get totally wrapped around the axle about what color to paint a room at our Zen center. I've gotten very upset myself at members of our community around questions of governance and changes in how we do things. Frankly, it can be discouraging to see those of us who devote so much time to manifesting a mindful, intimate life get entrapped by our emotions, entranced by our stories, and lash out, withdraw, or try to force control. But this is just what it is to be human, and this is in fact one of the best things about having a community of practice, a sangha.

Learning to deal with ourselves and others in a practice community allows us to grow. Audre Lorde once wrote, "Without community there is no liberation . . . but community must not mean a shedding of our differences, nor the pathetic pretense that those differences do not exist." If we don't have anyone who aggravates our reactivity as part of our practice, we'll never have the opportunity to face our harmful tendencies. Sure, it's possible to stop and be mindful and realize your connection to everyone at a meeting at your job when everyone is shouting or pouting, but it's really hard. If these problems come up at your Dharma center or church, however, there's a slightly better chance you'll remember that this moment of difficulty is your opportunity to practice awareness of the moment and intimacy with what's here. And if you do it, it will help. It will help you suffer less at the whims of your emotional conditioning and whatever stories your mind is telling you. It will help others suffer less, because you'll be less likely to throw fuel on the fire. It will help everything because it will put a few drops of goodness into the vast ocean of your habits and the conditioning of everyone and everything connected to your situation, which is ultimately the entire universe.

At first, it's probably best to focus on finding refuge in a sangha; then it's good to be open to working through some difficulties. Ultimately what's best is a balance that helps you to keep your feet on the path but encourages you to grow past your edges. You can cultivate this balance by entering a community simply: try to understand what the community is up to and flow into that. If it's supporting you, stick around. If not, it's probably time to look for another group. After a while, get more involved, help out with gardening or washing dishes. Avoid taking on too much authority or getting into decision-making early on. As you take on more activities you can use these as mindfulness practices, and thus train yourself to extend your present-moment peaceful awareness into more aspects of your life. I used to get annoyed when it was time to wash dishes at home, but now I generally enjoy it, because I practiced washing dishes at our Zen center. At some point if you stick around, someone might ask you to take more leadership. If your practice is stable and you feel a strong connection to your sangha, consider jumping in. Being on a nonprofit board is great practice. It can be hard, it can be inspiring, and it can be of great benefit to others. Bring your practice there. You can learn to be in the midst of complex issues and arguments with a peaceful heart, an open mind, and a sense that your intimacy with your peers and the entire world cannot be broken. Imagine if people carried this into families, governments, schools, and corporations.

12. Senses

My hands are typing, and the sound of rain pervades the air. Sitting on my porch in a soft blue chair, looking up to see leaves shaking in a light breeze and the weight of droplets landing and slipping away, I feel a chill. On the sidewalk, a man leans forward and tugs at his wandering dog's leash, hoping, I suppose, to get back indoors. Intimacy with our senses is a wonderful way to allow the mind to pause in its relentless machinations so that we can just be in life how it is.

Many of the things we enjoy the most call us into our senses: sunsets, landscapes, music, sex, sports, artmaking—the list is long. There are various things that people enjoy about these activities and experiences, but they share a common thread of calling us into the moment of sensing. People talk to me frequently about coming back refreshed after a few days in the natural beauty of woods, the mountains, or the desert. Many meditative traditions employ focus on sensory phenomena like a candle, breathing, or the sound of bells in order to still the activity of our thinking mind. The mind likes to have something to chew on, like a dog wants a stick. By giving it a sensory stick like a candle to gaze at, or the breath to focus on, or a series of yoga postures to pay attention to, or a deep forest to move through, we help it let go of the stick of rehearsing, reviewing, and reacting. This generally has a calming effect, which is good. We could all use a little calming.

Sight, sound, smell, taste, and touch—these are our five senses. If we are mindful of these senses they help us stay grounded in the present moment. The five senses only give us information now. The mind only gives us information now as well, but it convinces us that it can see the future or dwell in the past. The mind's ability to plan and learn from the past is very important, but it alienates us from our life in this very moment. So often its wonderful ideas of the future don't come to pass and we suffer, or we worry about something that never happens, or we chew on some past error or slight for far longer than could be of benefit. If we tune in to the senses, we can give the mind a break and wake up into how our life is now.

Practice: Mindfulness of the Senses

This practice can be done while sitting, cooking, or brushing the teeth, but I'll offer here instructions for cultivating mindfulness of the senses through walking meditation.

We begin by grounding awareness in the body and the breath—in the fifth sense of touch or bodily sensation. From this grounding we expand awareness into the other senses.

Notice how many steps you take with each breath, and then begin to follow the pattern. For example, draw awareness to the three steps you take while breathing in and the three steps you take as you breathe out.

From this basis, begin to expand your awareness to include sounds, sights, smells, and perhaps tastes. Allow the awareness to be broad.

If you find yourself absorbed in thought, return to the breath and pace, and then expand awareness to the other senses again.

Be mindful as awareness jumps from one element of your experience (squirrel!) to another (wind song). Be mindful as it narrows onto one object. From this mindfulness, gently encourage awareness to stay broad, including the whole range of sight, sound, smell, taste, and touch. Cultivate openness to a flowing panoramic awareness.

———————————————

There are various teachings on mindfulness of the senses in the *Four Foundations of Mindfulness Sutra*. The most fundamental is mindfulness of body, which appeared at the beginning of this book. Awareness of the sense of touch and of physical sensations in the body, particularly of the breath, is one of the most effective and powerful means of grounding oneself in the moment and realizing intimacy with life as it is.

The other teachings on mindfulness of the senses in the *Four Foundations of Mindfulness Sutra* are a little subtle and complex for this book. They emphasize first seeing how sensory experiences cause us to suffer and then learning how to let go of the clinging to sensory experiences that cause suffering. If mindfulness and intimacy with the senses are not done well and in balance with other practices, they can increase our suffering by making us more attached to pleasurable experiences. What we need is a practice that helps us know and be close to the senses without becoming attached to particular kinds of sensation.

I have eaten a spoonful of oatmeal during a meditation retreat that brought me to tears in wonder and gratitude. When people are deeply attuned to the moment and their senses, the simplest elements of life can be astonishing. Year after year people rave about the food that we serve at retreats at Minnesota Zen Meditation Center. But we just have a large cast of volunteer cooks, many of whom have very little cooking experience. I'm sure the mindfulness and care that we put into cooking makes a big difference, but the fact is that when you really pay attention, things are amazing. So many people step out of the meditation hall and walk down the street to see leaves and birds and faces as though they'd never seen anything like them before. As the Zen monk Hongzhi put it, "all things are inherently wondrous beyond description." This is what intimacy looks like; not knowing about something, but meeting it with an open heart, an open mind, and a sense of wonder.

So mindfulness of the senses can be wonderful and feel great. Just sitting in meditation, hearing the sound of rain on the roof and the soft shushing of planes high overhead. However, if we get great at mindfulness only when we encounter sensations we like, it won't help us all that much. We'll just want to keep coming back to that one time when the light was just right in the meditation hall and so silent, without these stupid people walking by and jabbering on the sidewalk outside. Instead of just knowing what it's like to eat an apple at our desk during work, we'll be imagining how great it will be to be deeply attuned to eating during the morning meal at our next retreat. The tough truth is, if you really want to find intimacy with your life, you need to be intimate with what happens in the senses whether you like it or not.

My first long Zen retreat was at Hokyoji Zen Practice Community in southern Minnesota. I chose to go somewhere surrounded by nature, at the bottom of steep wooded bluffs, away from phones and cars. During the week, I settled into the sounds of birds and rain, the array of greens across the valley. I ate the most amazing cookie I have ever eaten. It was sublime. And then the weekend came, with the start of deer season. For the rest of the retreat, every few minutes the sound of gunfire rocked the profound and meticulously maintained silence of our retreat. Sometimes I was annoyed, sometimes saddened, sometimes very amused, and often just present to the sensations of silence and sound and silence. As my teacher recommended, I kept returning to just knowing the sensory experience of now. I didn't change the practice of mindfulness of the senses when the senses gave me things I didn't like. I just let attention rest in what was there. I learned that I can be intimate with things I really don't like by drawing my awareness to the senses with mindfulness. As attunement to the senses increases, the reflexive judging of the mind softens. The mind-made aversion to sensations becomes less powerful than the actual vivid experience of being alive. I still prefer mindfulness of a subtle, simple miso soup to mindfulness of a cold, pelting rain, but by returning to both, I open the door to a joyful engaged intimacy with whatever I meet.

13. Nature

Outside my window I see green and yellow leaves. Leaves on the trees, leaves on the ground, leaves letting go and floating in the air. I've lived with the tree in front of my house for fifteen years, and it's steadily grown, without a lot of fuss, all this time. It doesn't look too worried about its leaves falling off on this cool, gray autumn day. Although these trees were planted and husbanded by human hands, they still show a natural order that goes far beyond any plans and desires a mind could ever make. Even in the city there is room to pause and connect with nature, and if we get out in the wild country we can find a connection to a vast realm of things growing and decaying together in a way that is both ancient and always exactly right now.

Just as there has been a lot of recent science showing that mindfulness promotes a wide array of mental and physical health benefits, there has been a similar body of research—with similar results—on spending time in nature. The effects have striking commonalities, including increased positive emotions, creativity, clarity of thought, and immune response, and decreased depression, anxiety, and inflammation. Historically, meditation and mindfulness have often been practiced in wild places: Buddha recommended going into the jungle or sitting at the foot of a tree, and in China hermits live high in the mountains away from the city to deepen their practice. The founder of Soto Zen, Dogen Zenji, regularly admonished his monks to leave the city and find a place to practice among the mountains and waters. I have practiced meditation outside on a regular basis for years. Sometimes I just sit in a local park, with the squirrels and ducks checking in to see if I've brought food, and other times I spend several days in the wilderness with all my gear in my backpack. I let nature show me something about living.

Nature calls us into our senses and, as I said in the previous chapter, the senses keep us grounded in the now. Nature also shows us a world that was not made for us, but of which we are made. If we want to realize intimacy, we need to see the world beyond our prejudices and desires, and nature shows us that world.

I find it helpful to sometimes take a minute to look around, wherever I am, and consider which things were made and put where they are in order to serve human wants, and which were not. For instance, from here in my study, the only thing I see that wasn't placed here according to human design is the sky. The desk, the laptop, the lights, the curtains, the window, and the road are all reflections in macro form of the discerning, judging, fixing capacity of human consciousness. The trees and grasses were placed there by human hands, but by their very nature they show some order and a way that is beyond our human ken. No one has managed to design a tree from scratch. Most people reading this spend most of their time relating to objects that were designed by human minds to serve human needs. Our sensory world is filled with material reflections of the judging, planning, and fixing aspect of our consciousness.

When we step out into nature or even take time to follow the movements of a squirrel running through the yard, we allow ourselves to meet a world that created us and that is far grander and more sublime than anything our worried minds will ever make. Stepping out onto a windswept prairie, gazing up at the black and stars, walking in the deep woods, gazing at the flow of a creek across a few moss-covered stones, climbing down into a valley or high on the side of mountain— these all open the door to realizing our intimacy with something infinitely beyond our conception. Real intimacy requires stepping beyond our habitual views. When you first look into a newborn's face, or at the Grand Canyon, what you see is the vastness of what you do not know and can't control. When you realize intimacy with another person is when you really open to what they are, beyond all your own ideas.

Realizing intimacy is about knowing a connection that already exists. Intimacy can't be forced or held on to; it is a condition of life of which we are either aware or ignorant. We sense this when we connect with the natural world. When we sense our intimacy with another person we feel with them: when they suffer, we suffer; when they feel joy, we can feel their joy. But this is always already true. I was very depressed in my early twenties, but I hid it pretty well. I had friends, I was a lot of fun at a party. Still, the pain in my heart affected everyone around me, from my quiet withdrawal from my family, to the small cruelties to my friends, to the bitterness in my interactions with strangers. I thought I could hide from intimacy, but it just wasn't true. Everything we do and everything we feel is intimate with everything already. Infinite conditions combine to impel us to feel and act, and our feelings and actions extend in all directions through cause and effect throughout all lives. Nature is the ground from which this whole human experience arises, and it is the milieu where our actions reverberate forever.

Natural selection produced these human forms, which we think are so different from other animal forms but are really just distant cousins. Watch a dog who is invited to go on a walk and then watch a child who is invited to go to a theme park, or watch yourself when you are invited to a marvelous concert. Watch ants in their orderly march from their ground nest to a discarded rind of fruit and then watch the cars cruising along the highways of a city. Watch a flower sprout, grow, bloom, and die, and then watch this happen to your loved ones. To see this we must be mindful of these things that we call *nature*. This will open the door to an intimacy that is already there.

Practice: Intimacy with Nature

There are many ways to cultivate intimacy with nature, but just finding natural spaces, plants, or animals and giving them your full, mindful attention is simple and wonderful. Watch birds without naming them; just see how they move. Take some time to sit among the trees, the grasses, or the desert sands. Let your mind soften, and let the natural world show you things that were not made *for* you but are made *with* you, that are your natural home.

From this sense of intimacy you can look into ways to enact intimacy, to *do* it. We are at a time when realizing our intimacy with the natural world is of urgent importance. Modern humans have tended to believe that we can view the world of nature as an object from which we are inherently separate, an object we can manipulate at will to serve our desires. This is a terrible way to try to have a relationship. It is also extremely dangerous, given that nature is of a power so vastly beyond ours. No one can stop a hurricane. The slabs of ice that are melting off the polar ice caps are of a size monumentally larger than any objects human technology can move. The human system of extracting what we want from the world is causing weather systems of immense power to change and animal and plant species to die at an astonishing rate. We are creating a situation in which staggering numbers of people may die due to climate change. It is time to let go of the idea that we can dominate and use nature, and to instead realize that we are intimate with it. Intimacy is not always easy. Ask any married couple. However, the alternative to intimacy is to deny its inescapable truth and retreat into a self-created alienation.

If we look at how our consumption affects the natural world, perhaps we can make some changes. We can support government, nonprofit, community, and corporate actions that support the natural world that is supporting us. Intimacy is how we are. We can cultivate our awareness, but ultimately intimacy is a path of action. The natural world is not done creating with us. It manifests our intimacy with dynamism and change in every moment, and with practice we can join in this creation from a sense of profound connection.

14. Blind Spots

Have you ever seen *King Lear*? As the play opens the king is aging, losing his strength and faculties, but he just can't see it. Everyone around him knows, but almost no one wants to tell him. They mostly want to take advantage of his weakness. Just one loving, strong-willed daughter is willing to tell him the truth—and oh, how he rages at her for it. Lear's lack of self-awareness and unwillingness to hear the truth sets the stage for one of literature's most wrenching tragedies. No matter how excellent our mindfulness practice is, no matter how attentive we are to our bodies, our emotions, and our thoughts, there will be parts of ourselves we just can't see, our blind spots. To get a more complete view we need to benefit from the mindfulness of others, their insight into who and how we are.

As a Zen teacher, one of my main jobs is to help people be aware of what is good in them, to hold a mirror up to all the wonderful things they do. I can't tell you how many times I've seen someone sitting on the cushion facing me look genuinely surprised when I pointed out something kind they had been doing. We all need reminders of the power we carry within us, day in and day out, to do something compassionate, something beautiful. Of course, if you want to support someone, sometimes it's helpful to bring up something that you see that they're doing that's *not* helpful. We all benefit from both kinds of feedback, but really it's good to weigh in on the good side. Most of us do a lot of good.

Personally, I enjoy positive feedback more than negative. I'd love to be that magical guy who just hears it all with total equanimity, but it isn't so. Still, I keep working on my ability to receive it all with an open heart and an open mind. Years ago, my barriers to intimacy were a lot thicker than they are now, and frankly, I thought I was a pretty awful person. When people would compliment me, or say something good about something I'd done, I'd deflect it with some sarcasm. When I was early in my path of recovery from addiction and mental illness, I remember deciding that I needed to get better at receiving people's insights into my blind spots. I recall practicing: standing behind the counter at work and hearing someone compliment what I was doing. It took a big effort to smile, take their message in, and simply say "thank you." I practiced receiving.

In those days, I'd meet negative feedback with defensiveness, lashing out, sulking, depression. It wasn't a lot of fun, but I've practiced at finding a better way. These days I can often thank someone for their input, even if it's quite unflattering, and take some time to consider whether their view can help me grow. If you want to be able to really grow from another's illumination of your blind spots, learn to be aware of your defenses. If anger, shame, complicated arguments, or ignoring come up, give them your attention and allow them to soften in the light of mindfulness. Then turn your attention to fully considering what you've heard.

However, receiving input with an open mind and without a lot of emotional reactivity does not mean that we passively accept whatever feedback we're given. A lot of the input we get about ourselves from other folks is wrong. Assertive women catch a lot of flak, people of African descent are inundated with the idea that they are inferior in countless ways, boys are told that if they are emotionally vulnerable they are weak. The list could go on for a long time. Ultimately, we have power to make choices that determine our character. If we have some mindfulness, some kind of discernment, of what kind of feedback we're getting, we are much more empowered to do something useful about it.

This part of the process isn't easy, and there are no rules. Generally, when it comes to feedback that shows you something you can't see about yourself, the more you trust someone, the more consistent the message, and the more people you hear it from, the more likely it is to be worth considering. For instance, I am very grateful that, despite all my resistance and denial, when a half dozen of my friends surprised me at our house as I was coming home from a night in county detox to ask me to go back to rehab and quit drinking, I heard their message, and I grudgingly acquiesced.

Unfortunately, sometimes we trust the wrong people, and sometimes the messages we get are just wrong. People in cults, people in unhealthy families, people with abusive partners, and all of us who are part of this culture with its many shortcoming are going to get feedback that is just wrong. You can bet that the great civil rights activist Rosa Parks had some folks telling her to quit rocking the boat. She stood firm, and I think it's clear that her wish will be realized: "To be remembered as someone who wanted to be free, so others would also be free." We are the ones who make the choice, but we can get some help to make it, and we can cultivate the ground to make it well.

Our blind spots are big. In Virginia Woolf's feminist classic *A Room of One's Own*, frustrated with women being held back from learning, she exclaims, "If through their incapacity to play football women are not going to be allowed to practice medicine—" One of the greatest minds of the twentieth century, and a seminal advocate for women's rights, didn't believe women could play soccer. Tell that to Mia Hamm! If this is true, must we not all be missing so much? What wondrous capacities do we not see in ourselves and others because of our prejudices?

For me, the best way to see through my biases has been listening to people who are different from me. For example, we have a growing and vibrant Somali American population in Minneapolis, where I live. Consciously, I've always been pleased and excited by this, but sometimes when being mindful of my emotions, I'd notice that I felt a subtle unease around big groups of Somali immigrants. I wasn't surprised; I grew up in a homogenous European American-dominated town and have a lifetime of negative images of Africans that I've received through the media. I worked on softening this unease with mindfulness, but by far the biggest change has come from hanging out in a coffee shop full of Somali folks watching football games, listening, contributing a bit, and gratefully receiving their warm hospitality. Lately, I've been following a local Somali politician who helps me to see ways in which my community holds people of color back. Just as we need friends and family to provide us feedback so we can see our blind spots, we need people from communities other than ours, particularly ones that have usually been marginalized, to help us see what we're missing. If we haven't developed the ability to hear negative feedback nonreactively, we may just keep holding people back.

Seek out people you trust whose judgment you trust. Listen to people who are different from you. Cultivate relationships with them where you can get feedback, good and bad. Practice receiving feedback with an open mind and without emotional reactivity. If reactivity is powerful, focus on taking care of it until it softens and then turn attention to seriously considering what you've heard. Try just saying "thank you" to feedback, good or bad. If you do this, you can let go of the reaction to the particular person, to your habitual response. Instead, in the light of mindfulness, you can test their opinion on the touchstone of your own heart, and from there choose your own way.

15. Possessions

Standing in line to buy groceries, I see magazines covered in ads. Scrolling through pages of thoughts shared by my friends, more ads drift by. Walking down the street, signs invite me in or direct me onward: buy, buy, buy. I think forward, hoping that on the weekend, I'll get some time to just relax with my family. I eat a big salad of locally grown vegetables for lunch and think about how this will help me get good health, perhaps long life. Sitting half lotus in the shifting shadows of dawn, I exhale and feel a subtle grasping as the mind waits for the moment when the body gets to hold some new air. Moment to moment throughout the day, I see phenomena inside and outside myself that call up a restless desire to acquire.

Acquiring wealth is among the most powerful driving values in America. Most people would not question that being able to have a more expensive car is better than having a cheaper one. *Cheap* is a word that historically means inexpensive or a good bargain, but in the last hundred years or so it has also come to mean contemptible, stingy, and just plain bad. The meaning of the word has changed in the United States as the value of having money has come to take a high seat among moral values like goodness and generosity. Expensive is good; cheap is bad. I met a woman a while back who recalled her usually mild-mannered father's outrage when President Jimmy Carter went on TV and put on a sweater and demonstrated turning down his thermostat to reduce fossil fuel use. Her father was appalled that someone would come on and suggest that he consume less. It was just flatly un-American!

We have many factors contributing to our culture of possession: within ourselves, our families, and our complex media culture. But this tendency for human beings to want to get stuff isn't new and in fact was central to why the Buddhist practices of mindfulness and intimacy came to be. The earliest Buddhist teachings, where mindfulness is so central, heavily emphasize the suffering caused by our obsession with "I, me, and mine." Intimacy, or interdependence, rose as a central value in later Buddhist teachings to counter the tendency of mindfulness practice to be used to get, to *acquire*, peace for oneself. The mindfulness and intimacy I'm teaching in this book is not designed to help you get anything. It is to help you give yourself to mindfulness practice so you may realize the intimate connection you already have with everything.

The first people to practice mindfulness were Buddhist monks and nuns. They had many practices aimed at letting go of the suffering involved in constantly trying to get stuff for themselves. They had almost no personal possessions: they had no homes, they didn't handle money, and they owned only clothing and a bowl with which they begged for and ate their only food. They practiced seeing nothing as being "I, me, or mine." They did this in both the way they spoke and in how they engaged in their mindfulness practice. Many of these people reported finding a freedom from suffering so vast it defied description, but they tried describing it anyway, because they wanted to share it with us. The first book I wrote was a commentary on an eighth-century Zen poem, "Song of the Grass-Roof Hermitage." The poem begins:

> I've built a grass hut where there's nothing
> of value.
> After eating, I relax and enjoy a nap.

The author, Shitou, was carrying forward the ancient tradition of living simply formed by those early monks, and his poem describes a life of joyful ease and connection in the midst of nature, with almost no possessions. Living in the mountains in a grass hut, eating gathered wild plants and occasional offerings from the surrounding community, may sound crazy or wonderful to you, but the truth is, I doubt either of us is going to do it. But what it shows us is that a wondrous life of harmony with your surroundings is available with almost no stuff.

The last thing I want to do here is make anyone feel ashamed about having stuff or wanting stuff. I have stuff, I want stuff; it's part of the human deal. However, I think it is worth questioning, over and over again, how having stuff and wanting stuff affects our lives and the lives around us. It can be very helpful to just be mindful of the words "I, me, and mine." If a waiter forgets to bring a cup of tea you ordered and you say, "he forgot my tea," how does it make you feel? What does it mean for a cup of tea that has never been made, that does not exist, to be "my tea"? Just notice when you use these words and notice how they feel. Then perhaps dive into the question of what they really mean.

Practice: Mindfulness of Possessives

With meditation practice we can be mindful of things that we might normally think of as "mine." When you are sitting, observe and perhaps even question the things you think of as "yours": Is there an ache in your foot, or do you have an ache, or is it an ache in a foot? Are the thoughts arising and fading yours, are they you? What are you sitting on: a cushion or your cushion?

It can also be interesting to try to avoid using the term

mine. My yoga teacher always says "raise the left leg" rather than "raise your left leg." She uses language like this to help soften our sense of "mine," to help us let go. If we don't hold on to the idea of "mine" it really helps us to relax and see what's here. We don't have to try to keep what we've got and get the next thing we want.

———————————

There are people who argue that if everyone is focused on getting things for themselves, it works out well for everyone. This does not reflect my experience on a personal or community level, or my sense of what is happening in the big wide world. My life used to be very focused on getting what I wanted, and it was miserable and lonely. The more I focus on cultivating intimacy with the present moment, myself, and my friends and family, the happier I've been. Musical groups I've been in where people became focused on getting things their way fell apart—and frankly they didn't sound very good. Groups where people were focused on the common goal of creating something great to offer to the world were a joy to be in, and they often produced something quite wonderful. The United States, with its abiding sense that acquiring and having wealth is inherently and profoundly beneficial, is a country where a lot of people are unhappy and alone, where drug and alcohol addiction is rampant, where our massively disproportionate consumption of natural resources has a terrible impact on billions of people in less wealthy countries—an impact that is only getting worse with global climate change.

None of us can wave a magic wand and change the vast cultural, personal, and economic systems that drive this destructive fascination with possession. However, we can be aware of it, we can be intimate with our feelings about it. We can let that awareness and intimacy open up questions of how and why we consume things. If we really look at this deeply we can see that our own desires are not so unlike other people's. We can recognize our shared burden of thinking that having stuff is going to keep us safe and happy. Knowing that we carry this together, we can begin to try different ways for ourselves, we can share the challenges we have with others, we can see one more way in which we are all as one.

16. Family

We learn about intimacy as children. Wrapped in a towel after a bath and laughing, lying sleepy in bed as someone tells an oft-told story, freezing in fear as an angry parent rails, getting out of trouble by making everyone laugh, lying to avoid the shame of admitting a mistake, holding hands as we cross the street. It's a mixed bag. Everyone's experience is different, but much of our sense of intimacy comes from deeply embedded emotional and cognitive habits formed from these early experiences. Some of us grow up in a generally safe and happy environment, and intimacy usually seems easy and sweet. On the other hand, I had a dear friend whose parents were angry and distant when she was young. She had to work bravely and mightily to be able to find intimacy with people that felt safe and joyful. It was a struggle to grow beyond the powerful early impressions of intimacy as a place of danger and aloneness. Most of us lie somewhere in the middle, and all of us have gaps in our ability to trust and be close to our loved ones. However, our sense of intimacy is always developing, and we can practice to find a deeper and healthier sense of closeness to those around us.

Practice: Mindfulness with Family

If you want to grow in your capacity for intimacy, the first step is to regularly check in with how you feel about it. When you are with your family, just pause occasionally, take three mindful breaths, and notice how you feel. Do this when you think things are going well and also when you think they're not.

Many Western psychotherapy models would involve thinking about how your present feeling relates to your early childhood feeling and memories; when we're small our emotional habits begin to form and they have a strong tendency to repeat themselves. This is very helpful, and I highly encourage you to consider some form of psychotherapy if you'd like to be happier and healthier. However, for this mindfulness practice, all we need to do is actually give nonjudgmental, compassionate awareness to the feeling. This way we keep it simple, but we access the enormous power of mindfulness of emotions.

Mindfulness enables us to touch the heart of our early impressions of intimacy, but intimacy goes beyond how we feel about our families when we're little. The people in our families when we were young were young once too, so their early senses of intimacy inform how they treat us and how we are formed. Just like us, their relationships to intimacy are dependent on choices and attitudes throughout their lives, and all kinds of media, stories, and advice from countless sources, all of which got their senses of intimacy from an equally vast and endless array of places. Your experience of intimacy is already interdependent with everything. Even when you feel most cut off from everyone, when intimacy seems impossible, that feeling is a manifestation of your intimacy with everything.

It's good to realize, to feel, to enact the intimacy with everything that we already have, that we already are. We can cultivate this capacity with two mindfulness practices. First, we allow mindfulness of body to help us know safety, empowerment, and groundedness. Second, we use mindful listening to open up awareness and learn to be truly present to those around us. It's best to develop these capacities in sitting meditation, but they are also available right in your home with your family.

When we practice mindfulness of body and breath, many things happen, but over time we will begin to shed, or at least take a break from, the stories our mind is making that make us anxious and angry. The mental habits that we have formed as protection against difficult feelings and potential problems are weakened as awareness rests in the feelings of the body breathing. So this practice helps us cultivate a sense of safety. If we stick with it we will also see that all kinds of feelings and thoughts arise, some lovely and some painful, and we can learn that no matter what they are, no matter how difficult or intense, we can just sit there with them and be present. We can realize a profound empowerment, the empowerment of not being driven by these habits of feeling and thought that formed through infinite time, the empowerment of just knowing how we are and making a choice in this moment. I encourage you to review the practice of mindfulness of body in chapter 4.

If you cultivate this capacity in sitting meditation you will be able to access it in your daily life with your family. When you are frantically trying to get everyone to get in the car and go somewhere, you can pause, know the breath and the body, and realize you don't have to be driven by the fear of being late, by the shame of thinking your family is in chaos. You can find a safe, empowered space to calmly do the next right thing. When you are sitting on the couch with a child and realize you aren't listening to them at all, but rather planning your day, you can pause and return to the body and breath, and realize your anxiety doesn't have to run your life, and you can just be present and intimate with your child. When you are arguing and shouting, or perhaps silently stewing about a fight with your wife, your child, or your father, you can stop, know the breath and the body, and see if your life really is in danger—maybe you don't have to freak out quite so hard; you have the power to pause and choose something beneficial that isn't just what your conditioned mind came up with out of emotional habit.

The practice I've been talking about is finding a boundary. Finding a boundary between yourself and all the thoughts and external senses, and checking in with the body and emotion. It's a very brief retreat into a safe space you create. It may not always feel safe—your feelings will still be there—but with practice you can learn to know that is actually *is* safe to be with your body's energy. You can find you have the strength and courage to be with however you feel.

Of course, the situation in your family may actually *be* dangerous, or so emotionally fraught that the best thing to do is to get away. Remember that mindfulness is about developing your ability to choose what is most beneficial, and remember you don't have to do it alone. If things are really overwhelming there is help, and taking care of yourself is fundamental.

If we want to realize the joy, the freedom, the pure out-and-inflow of compassion that is boundaryless intimacy, we need healthy boundaries first. Cultivating a sense of safety and empowerment is fundamental. But if we have this sense to some degree, we can begin to cultivate boundarylessness. There are many roads to this, but in your family life, one of the best ways is to practice mindful listening. In this case mindful listening includes all the senses, pouring compassionate nonjudgmental awareness into hearing the people in your family.

Practice: Mindful Listening

It's good to practice mindful listening when you are sitting in meditation. Just focus awareness on whatever sound arises without naming or figuring out what you are hearing, returning attention again and again to the field of sound as the mind wanders away. If you do this, you will likely feel that you are sensing a larger space, that you have expanded the boundary of awareness.

If you cultivate this capacity you can share it with your loved ones, and you will see how this begins to soften the boundary between you and them. You will see how it opens up space for intimacy. When you are distracted from your loved ones by the churnings of your mind, just pause and listen to them. You may find that countless opportunities to share the joy of life with your loved ones are right in front of you. When you are in conflict, or they are unhappy, it is not so easy to do. But remember, one of the reasons you are in conflict and they are unhappy is that your shared sense of intimacy has become weak, you all feel cut off, alone. The teenager jams in the earbuds the minute they see you, the father turns up the car radio during the first moment the family is in the same space together, the wife demands that things be done just so. You are the one who can stop and take time to listen with your whole heart. You have the power and the strength to listen without judgment to an angry sibling. If you don't think you have it, you can cultivate it; just keep trying. When you listen with your whole heart, it doesn't mean you have to agree with what another person says. It just means you care enough to pay attention. Intimacy is the harmony of difference and sameness. You can be absorbed in the field of listening, in the field of awareness, in the vast unfolding of the world, and you can choose to be present and cultivate connection.

Intimacy with family can be so vast, open, and joyous that it knows no bounds. I recall a story from my Zen teacher Tim Burkett: He had picked a small bowl of wild strawberries in the woods near his home and was sitting with his wife and son having breakfast. The berries were rare and wonderful. He doled out one-third of the berries to each. Tim savored them, his little son loved them, his wife ate one and gave the rest to their son. Tim said, "Linda, you hardly got any." She said, "Yes, but they tasted so good."

17. Friends

I recall with profound gratitude the daily deliveries of food from my family's friends as my father entered his last living days. My mother, my brother, and I stayed in the house grieving, reminiscing, loving, doing our best to ease the last days of my father, whose body was racked with the pain of cancer, whose mind was faced with a vast unknown, and whose heart was full and strong. I learned so much in those days, but in particular I learned something about friendship: how there are many ways to be a friend.

My father had some close friends, those people with whom he shared his inner world, parts of himself that weren't for public view. He had many friends with whom he shared values and good times, conversations at parties and after concerts. He had colleagues, with whom he was not so close, but with whom he shared his deep commitment to his work. These people were all there for us when he was near life's end. They were there in various ways that matched the kind of friendship that they'd had, but it was clear with each meal delivered that what we were seeing was intimacy in action. Friends with whom he had a more private, personal bond would find their way to his side, to sit with him and share life as they had done so many times. Other friends, perhaps from a more public sphere, would almost shyly come to the door, hand us some food, perhaps give a hug, and head on home. They knew we needed support, and they knew the best expression of intimacy, of love, was a gift of something practical and space for our family to grieve.

We can find a deep personal intimacy with a close friend, and we can find a broader sense of intimacy with all those friends we don't know quite so well, but who enrich our lives in their own way. If you have close friends with whom who you can share the deep, difficult, and wondrous parts of your life, that is wonderful. If you don't, that is just fine too, but it's worth being open to the possibility. Many of us would like to have some people like this, but we can't quite figure out how to do it. The thing is we can't just *decide* to have great friends. For one thing, in a friendship, two people come together, and that's not something one person can make happen. For another thing, friendship, like romantic love, is a little mysterious. Out of all the people we encounter, why do we form close bonds with some of them? Although you may be able to list some reasons, to some extent, this coming together is beyond our ken.

We can, however, cultivate the ground for friendship. Being mindful when listening to people is a great start. You can do this with a stranger you're standing next to at a fireworks display in the dark of the Fourth of July, and you can do it with a friend you've known since you were little kids running through a sprinkler on a hot day. Just giving your attention is the basis for the possibility of connection. Being curious really helps. Focusing your attention on understanding and learning about someone is an act of intimacy. Letting them show you what they feel comfortable with is key. Once you're trying to extract information or trying to force a connection, it's not intimacy anymore; it's just self-centered need. If you find yourself going down this road, the best thing is to focus mindfulness on your own sense of need and take care of yourself.

For friendships to be healthy they need to be reciprocal. We need to hear and be heard, we need to support and be supported. We need to develop our sense of what kind of intimacy our friends want, and understand and respect what feels right for ourselves. It's good to be a leader—to be the first to send an invitation to a barbecue or a knitting circle, to be vulnerable, to make space for someone to be vulnerable, or to bring some soup to an ailing friend—but if people don't want to reciprocate it's good to just give them space.

There isn't some correct amount of friends or way to do friendship, but friendship is one of the most natural ways human beings experience intimacy, so it's worth our attention. A little mindful investigation of what our sense of friendship looks like is great.

Practice: Mindfulness of Friendship

Take a stroll. Just walk and breathe for a bit. Or if you cannot walk, find a chair and be still. Find the breath in the body, in harmony with your steps if you're walking.

Take some time to think about friends you've had, or have, or would like to have. Notice how you feel.

Think of things you value in friendship, like fun, connection, or comfort. Notice how you feel.

Take some time to consider things you could do to make room for more of what you value in friendship in your life. Don't be too ambitious, just be open. Notice how you feel.

Be open to change, to ideas about how to cultivate good friendship, but don't force it.

By cultivating friendships, we can find a way to deepen our sense of being supported, and we can find the joy and empowerment of supporting others. We can see that these are not two things. It became so clear each evening in the fading days of my father's life, as I'd answer the door to look in the eyes of another friend who'd hand me a hot plate of dinner, that they felt grateful to be able to give something, and I was grateful to receive it.

18. Romance and Sex

How many songs are there about the towering heights of romance, of an overwhelming connection with another? How many songs about the wrenching heartache of separation from the beloved? Movies, one of the most central ways of storytelling in our modern age, have all kinds of plots, but so many end with a kiss, the union of two loved ones whose painful separation drove our need to see the story through to the end. Folktales, plays, novels, and poems for thousands of years and across cultures have been dominated by this simple story arc: lovers were not together and they came together. The desire for intimacy through romantic involvement and sex is a big deal.

I've spent a fair amount of time watching animals. I've watched squirrels, ducks, wildebeests, and bighorn sheep chasing and fighting to establish mates. In spring, the carp in the lake by my home thrash wildly in the shallows, hurling their bodies out of the water in the struggle to find partners, and I've had a couple sleepless nights as cats enacted the yowling, painful ritual of their mating. We are not alone in the drama or the power of this coming together.

Of course, we can have romance without sex or sex without romance. By *romance* I mean the kind of relationship that usually involves physical attraction and a strong attachment to another, the kind of relationship where you might go on dates, live together, or get married. Sometimes we find deep, wondrous intimacy in the realms of sex and romance, and other times we don't. For many people I know, some of the most painful experiences we have are those where we lost the sense of intimacy within a romantic relationship. And sexual intimacy can be consummately fulfilling, but it can also be hollow and disappointing or even alienating and painful.

I suspect that a few people picked up this book thinking that it would solely be about using mindfulness to improve one's romantic relationships. So many stories and songs and so many other elements of our culture tend to concentrate on the impulse to connect, to find intimacy, toward monogamous romance. These kinds of relationship are a beautiful and valuable place to cultivate intimacy, but this book is really here to help show that the yearning we have to find intimacy can be fostered and harnessed so that it informs every aspect of our lives and every type of relationship we have. Nonetheless, we will spend a little time in the realm of romance and sex; because there is so much of our sense of intimacy wrapped up in it, it is a very powerful ground for practice.

The range of experience we humans have around romance and sex is quite large. I've known people who found someone they loved, got married, and had a close relationship for the rest of their lives. Others have few or no lovers. Some people have sex with lots of people they never know all that well. Some have many committed relationships. All of these are accompanied by a wide range of joys, boredoms, sufferings, and dramas. This is not the book to tell you which one is best. This is the book to tell you to bring mindfulness into the realm of romance and sex and to never give up the aspiration to open up to and express a greater sense of intimacy.

Whether you have been married for years, you are searching for someone, you are in the throes of a fresh romance, you're just not interested, or you are so brokenhearted that intimacy seems like a game for fools, you do have room to grow *and* you do have something to offer. It is very easy for us humans to act out of habit. We barely know we're doing it, and it can be very hard to change. With mindfulness we can know our selves and our motivations and actions just a little better, and intimacy allows the change to happen in a harmonious way.

Do we really understand why we love the people we do? Do we actually know why we keep having the same kinds of fights with our spouses or choosing to be in relationships where we are unfulfilled in the same old ways? There is a lot of mystery to this whole thing, and we can let it rest in the realm of mystery, but I encourage you to begin to tune in to what you feel and what you choose in a mindful way. This won't explain this mystery, but it will enable you to make a choice in the moment not just based on impulse and habit. As you might expect, practicing meditation on a regular basis will greatly increase your capacity to be mindful about your romantic relationships. But here I will suggest some key times to tune in.

Practice: Mindfulness in Relationships

Whenever you are aware of strong feelings or notice a lot of thought directed toward a romantic partner or the possibility of finding one, just stop, take three mindful breaths, and briefly concentrate your attention on how you feel. Whether the feeling is good or bad does not matter; it's just good to know it, to have some sense that this feeling is intimately connected with what you are thinking and what you will do.

Whenever you are about to do something of note in the realm of romance, ask yourself, "Why am I doing this?" Try to answer from your heart. Don't write an essay, just notice what's behind the impulse to act: affection, desire, anger, fear, or compassion. Take a moment, again, to tune in to the emotional tone that underlies your actions.

I have found over time that if I'm acting out of anger or neediness, I usually make a mess of things, so I often wait to act if that's the emotion I find when I check in. If you're going to ask someone out, it's good to check in and know why. If you're bringing flowers home for your wife, is it just to share joy or because you are afraid she'll still act distant? As you become more mindful of the feelings that underlie and drive your life you will find that you are freer to choose based on your values rather than your impulses.

Another great way to bring mindfulness into your relationships is to practice mindful listening. Yesterday, I heard from a number of students who'd been trying it with their spouses for a week. The results were pretty amazing. They were smiling and laughing and sharing how surprised they were at how good it felt, how it opened things up. They'd all been married for years and all they really did to make this change was pay attention! One large scientific study I saw recently posited that nothing is a more effective indicator of relationship satisfaction than how often partners respond attentively when their partners request attention.

Practice: Mindful Listening with Others

If you want to listen mindfully to someone, orient your whole body toward listening, stop all other activities, let go of your own ideas, and pour your attention into hearing and understanding. You don't have to figure anything out. You won't be engulfed or erased by just hearing. You can choose to be all ears for a little bit, and then you can go back to whatever you'd like. If this seems hard, try doing it once a day. If it seems easy, try doing it every time you are addressed. If it's your first date, see if you can let go of proving you are worthy or getting something out of the date and just *hear*, just really *meet*.

Mindful listening is a great open door to intimacy. You can meet another with pure presence, not with ideas, desires, or worries. I've known couples wrapped in long, painful, intractable arguments who found peace, connection, and resolution when they finally found a way to just hear and understand each other. I've seen couples who were doing fine, just getting along, whose relationship found new depth when they actually stopped to pay attention to each other. We all probably know what it's like to have a conversation in which someone is focused on getting something from us. Doesn't it feel better when people are there to just know us as we are, with listening? We may even be able to admit that sometimes we're that person who isn't really listening but is just waiting to talk. We can always take the conversation we're in as a moment to really connect.

We can also find deep connection in sex. Sometimes, sadly, we do not. Attitudes toward sex are quite various and rapidly changing here in the modern, tumultuous West. One friend put it pretty well in a Buddhist teen group: "Sex can be wonderful, and sometimes it makes people crazy." Repressing sexuality is dangerous. Uncontrolled sexuality is also dangerous. I recommend honoring, enjoying, and respecting your own sexuality and making a commitment to express it in ways that harm no one and promote intimacy.

My attitude here is in definite contrast with many spiritual and religious teachings, including some of the Buddhist teachings from which this book arises. A lot of ancient and even recent teachings on sexuality recommend a great deal of repressing of sexual feelings and actions. I recommend minimizing repression, as I trust modern sex research and the stories of people I know, which suggests it is harmful. In recent years people have become more honest about their sexual lives, and I trust the intimacy and awareness that comes from this honesty.

It is important to acknowledge that research shows that many, if not most, people's internal erotic lives are wilder and more transgressive than we'd generally admit. It is very common for people to find things erotically charged that they would almost never share with another person. It is also common for people to have aspects of their sexuality that they would never enact: taboo things or even violent things. It is difficult and dangerous to pretend we don't have these aspects of ourselves. The human sexual mind is mysterious and powerful, so it's important to be mindful and know that these aspects of our erotic imagination exist.

If we are willing and able to acknowledge the erotic aspects of our experience, we are on a better footing to act in a way that is truly healthy—healthy for everyone. Imagine a Venn diagram with your values in one circle and things you find erotic in the other. The overlapping area is a good place to locate your sexual behavior. Imagination, fantasy, and masturbation are a safe place to play with the aspects of your erotic mind that don't fit with your values. If you really love someone and share a committed relationship, I recommend that you be brave in opening up to them about what gets you going. Just being honest about something so personal is an act of intimacy. It may or may not become a part of a shared sexual life, but it may open the door for a deeper connection.

The intimacy we can find with a sexual partner can be wondrous. We share parts of our bodies that usually no one sees, sharing aspects of ourselves that are usually so hidden. We can disappear into the joy of shared pleasure. We may revel in being able to make another feel so good, in allowing someone else to please us so completely. If we get caught thinking this is the only way we can experience deep intimacy it can be a terrible trap, but if we pay attention we may allow the intimacy and openness of shared sex to show us how to be more open and intimate with the joy and pleasure of living.

Perhaps there are ways in which you express your sexuality that harm people, or you fear that the erotic play of your mind will drive you to do something harmful. It is important to find ways to manage behavior without shaming or attacking our internal erotic drivers; shame and repression make the harmful energy come out in more insidious ways. If you are overly promiscuous or assiduously avoid sex, there may be some excellent opportunities to be more mindful and intimate with yourself, to learn about why you choose what you choose. Be present to what is in you, and from that choose a better way. Because sexuality is so private, if it is unhealthy, it really helps to get it into the open. If there are aspects of your sexual life that are harmful or painful, it's really good to find professional help to work with it, to share the act of caring for and healing these powerful energies. You don't have to suffer alone. It's important to acknowledge that sexual violence is common but has often been unspoken. Survivors have been standing up lately, bringing truth where there has been silence. Their courage opens a path for us all to change.

Research shows that it is rare for married couples to find commonality in their most taboo erotic interests, and yet many couples find tremendous connection and intimacy in sex. If you could get any given couple to be honest enough to make a Venn diagram of what they each find sexy, the overlap is likely to be pretty modest. But the simple act of sharing and honesty can create great intimacy, and what common ground there is can be amazing to explore together. Sexual union can bind us powerfully to the beloved. Here the first definition I gave of intimacy comes in handy: realizing the harmony between our differences and our connection. I encourage you to turn toward the capacity of sex to be a place of profound connection, of completely giving ourselves to our lovers, our activity, and ourselves.

19. Work and Play

Have you ever looked up from your workspace and realized you barely remember the last five minutes of working, because your mind was so full of thoughts about something else? Or perhaps you've had moments when you are keenly aware: completely pouring yourself into the activity at hand, absorbed in creating the perfect database query, hearing a client with your whole being, crafting each fragrant piece of lumber into the perfect frame for a door.

Watching adults working and watching children at play we can see common themes as well as differences. In the creative phase of a project what we do is in many ways similar to what I hear the kids doing at the daycare next door, making up a game as they go, "Now, I'm getting into my submarine." "OK, I'll go get my scuba tanks!" A lot of work looks kind of like a sport: everyone lines up according to the rules, people laugh, they get frustrated, they win and lose, they feel the pain of losing and the pleasure of winning, they make friends, and they make enemies. One of the biggest differences between work and play, however, is our attitude. People tend to like playing more than they like working.

You might argue that this is because we take our work too seriously. I don't think so. Those kids I hear through the window running around the yard and shouting are not messing around. They are seriously absorbed in whatever adventure they are creating, but they don't seem to be worried about what they're going to get out of it. They don't spend a lot of time planning it, and when it's over they're on to the next thing. If you want to find the joy of play in work, the most important thing is to focus more on what you are doing than on the outcome. If you are focused on the moment's task, it's going to feel better than thinking about how soon you'll get done. If your mindset is "another day, another dollar," you sacrifice your life now for an outcome, for something later. Professional sports show an area where work and play overlap. How well I remember seeing a player who focuses intensely on winning crushed and dejected under the glare of lights, looking down at his feet, and mumbling through an interview. And then there is the exultant glow of the winners. We'll all end up on both sides of this coin. What I find inspiring is those players who in the heat of intense competition pop up from a mistake with a smile but also an obvious commitment to come back and do their best again, and those who in the heat of confrontation pause to lean down, stick out a hand, and help a player from the other team up. You can see that they are alert to what is happening right in that very moment, not just who will win the game.

Finding ways to offer your attention to your work activities can expand your life. It will bring a quality of play into your work. It will also create some cracks in your sense that your work is separate from the rest of life. You can begin to see that whether you are at work or not, you are just where you are, with some kind of new, never-before-seen experience unfolding. However, if we really want to dive beyond mindfulness and touch a greater intimacy, we'll need to do more than just pay attention to our current activity.

Holistic mindfulness is, in the earliest and most central Buddhist teaching, one of eight elements of a path toward nonsuffering and well-being: holistic view, intention, speech, action, livelihood, effort, mindfulness, and concentration. These elements are intended as an integrated system of wellness. If we're really interested in being well, and finding intimacy with all things, we should investigate our work. What we do, what we produce, and where we put our time are already involved in an infinitely complex web of interconnection. Your job is already intimate with everything. It's worth learning about and enacting this intimacy intentionally.

When I first began providing mindfulness training to police officers, I had the great fortune to meet with one of the pioneers of this kind of work, the late Cheri Maples. Cheri was a police captain in Madison, Wisconsin, who had a transformative experience at a retreat led by the beloved Vietnamese Zen monk Thich Nhat Hanh. She continued practice with him, and eventually he ordained her. She told me that there were folks who criticized him for ordaining a person who carried a gun at work, and he said, "Why wouldn't you want the people carrying guns to be mindful?"

The earliest texts on holistic livelihood in the Buddhist tradition say not to engage in the sale or making of weapons, meat, slaves, sex workers, drugs, or alcohol. The idea was that these industries are among the most harmful. Nowadays, however, we live in a staggeringly complex economy; one corporation that manufactures weapons may also make life-saving medicines. Because the interconnection is so great, it can be hard to know what a holistic way to make a living is. Also, for many people, finding a job is hard, and we have lives and maybe dependents to support. If we have a lot of flexibility in how we make a living, it's important to acknowledge that this is a privilege many people can't access.

All that said, we should learn about and engage in how our livelihood connects to the rest of the world. This book is not about telling you exactly what to do, and these teachings are not about you figuring out what other people should do. But please take time to consider how your livelihood affects people in your family, your neighborhood, the rest of the country, and all over the world, as well as the animals on the ground and the trees, the sleek fish of the seas, geese flying, trees, grasses, bees, and the very earth out of which all this life is born. Out of this consideration, let the path of your work life flow.

I don't have a specific path in mind, and I know that it can be very hard to find work that feels like it truly expresses your sense of connection. Considering holistic livelihood isn't about achieving a specific result; it's about investigating your values and keeping an open mind. Life is big. Open your heart to possibility, and have a kind respect for your own need to make a living. I know and love folks who work for nonprofits or for the government, who do manual labor, who work as lawyers, people who struggle to find work or can't work due to disability, corporate executives, artists, musicians, dancers, stay-at-home moms and dads. We each have to find our way.

I recall a story one friend told me. She was working at a huge corporation dealing with payroll, sending out paychecks to thousands of employees. She felt troubled that her work wasn't really contributing to the greater good and confided in a friend. Her friend said, "Imagine if all those people didn't get their paychecks. They couldn't buy food, or pay for their kid's piano lessons, or go to visit their parents." We are connected, our intimacy is inescapable; keep looking for it. It's always there, in work or in play.

20. Ritual

How well I remember the face of my young son, shining and expectant, as he walked down the aisle of a church to receive his first communion. How many times have I given a wholehearted bow to the altar at Minnesota Zen Center as I prepared to light the candle before meditation? Even now I can see the tears streaming down an athlete's face as he held his hand on his heart and sang the national anthem, and the stoic resolve of another as he knelt for the same song. Lord, how it touched my heart when I turned a corner in the gray and beige hallway of a hospital addiction rehab unit and saw the enraptured faces of two old women in wheelchairs being rolled into a dim-lit chapel. Ritual contextualizes and makes communal our most powerful emotions. It helps us find intimacy in the realms of our lives where we can sometimes feel so alone.

When we attend a play or a movie, we all engage in a ritual of coming together and offering our attention in a ritual space to share and feel an experience, to gasp together and to laugh together, and sometimes to cry together. We might not be so open to let our feelings and responses flow without the ritual container of the theater. You may laugh at those who shout and leap from their chairs at sports events, at those anxious, rally-capped faces hunched toward their TVs in the ninth inning—or you may be one of them. Either way, people are manifesting their shouting and leaping energies, their deep sense of concern, in a way that seems appropriate and safe to them. Like sports fans, people go to church and birthday parties in part because they want to feel connected at the level of the heart.

Ritual can be a wonderful way to cultivate our sense of intimacy and connection with our communities, our spiritual beliefs, and our selves. Mindfulness is a valuable complement to the intimacy of ritual. It allows us to both deepen ritual's power to help us know ourselves—and to deal with the dark side of ritual.

You can find many images of lynching in the United States—a huge crowd of white men surrounding a black man's corpse. The ritual of the execution of black men by white men solidified and expressed the sense of connection between the whites and their alienation from the blacks. Iterations of rituals where people come together to sense their connection in relation to their fear, hatred, or desire for power are myriad and horrific. The legacy of this violence lives within us, as does the capacity to heal it. The work of healing the trauma of the African American community and dismantling the conscious and unconscious racism of European Americans is ongoing. We are not separate from this deep and dangerous aspect of human behavior; we are in fact intimately connected with it, just as we are to all of life.

I pray that no one reading this would ever do anything so appalling as racially motivated murder, but there might be countless smaller, more mundane ways we allow ritual to separate ourselves from others. Men make sexist jokes at meetings; crowds of baseball fans do the "tomahawk chop" with caricatures of Native American faces on their shirts. Maybe we meet weekly with friends to talk trash about others. At a political rally what do we do? To paraphrase Michelle Obama, do we go low, or do we go high? The power and appeal of ritual lives in us in ways we may never know. However, we can cultivate mindfulness of our tendency to find both intimacy and alienation in ritual. With this mindfulness we can create ritual that doesn't separate, that encourages intimacy with all of life, with everything.

Practice: Mindfulness During Ritual

Begin with mindfulness of your emotions during ritual; just notice and identify the range of feelings. Not judging, just giving them compassionate presence. Maybe you're someone who likes to meditate but gets hives anytime someone bows in a meditation group. When people start chanting you want to jump up and get out of there. People can have very strong emotional reactions to ritual; just notice what yours are. When you are at a graduation ceremony, don't just cry as a disabled student slowly makes her way across the stage; give some real attention to the feeling you are experiencing. If you are in church or at a movie, know the range of feelings: Is there love and connection? Is there anger, shame, or fear? Just stay present and honest with how you are and let your feelings flow.

––––––––––––––––

This way of mindfulness can be very revealing, for you can see that if there are painful or negative emotions, something usually seems cut off. When there is fear, the mind will find an object to fear; when there is shame, the mind will make an image of you that is not good enough to fit in with the world. This is a normal aspect of being human, driven by emotion: our mind is constantly creating this sense of separation. That tendency is not an enemy; it is intimately connected to what it is to be alive. Ritual, however, is an excellent context for us to work with this tendency, to learn about it and to soften its hard edges. Ritual both elevates our most powerful emotions, our feelings of connection and separation, and also makes a safe context for us to experience them.

Oftentimes it's good to let yourself be swept away

during ritual and let the experience flow. Let the feelings, the sounds, and the motions just be as they are. Let them call you into the moment. Let the ritual do what it does: make space for you to fully feel in a safe, connected context. It's important, however, to occasionally bring in mindfulness and check in with how the ritual actually feels. We want to know how well our ritual is fostering our sense of connection and how much it is creating a sense of separation. With this awareness we can, over time, shift the kinds of rituals we engage in to those that help us process our feelings and help us feel closer to life, rather than those that ramp up feelings we don't need and cut us off.

If you notice in the context of a ritual that some person, group of people, institution, or anything at all is pushed outside of the circle of your connection, you could consider bringing them in. If not, consider whether another ritual might serve you better, or at least try to bring some lightness to the whole thing. A little awareness can go a long way in bringing this lightness. Our psyches need safe ritual spaces to process our more dangerous impulses and painful emotions. I recall one prominent Buddhist teacher saying that every once in a while he just needed to go see an action movie and let himself experience all that dramatic violence. Ritual can provide a safe, appropriate outlet for our need to feel there's an "us" and a "them." We should remember, however, that the guys on the baseball team you don't like are not actually evil. It may be fun to watch Scarlett Johansson throw a bad guy off a building in the climactic fight of a movie, but see if you can remember there aren't actually any bad guys here; that's all actors and make believe.

Drug and alcohol use often take ritual forms. Marijuana smokers sit in a circle, junkies arrange their paraphernalia just so, drinkers raise a toast. A toast at a wedding can be so lovely, so inspiring, but with alcohol sometimes things go terribly wrong. The connection to a community through a shared drink is about finding intimacy, and so is an addict's lonely ritual of finding communion with a fleeting high. These show in stark contrast the good and bad of ritual. If you know addiction you know it's hard to break, and if you have seen the racial history of the United States you know that racism is hard to break. To break them, and countless other systems of suffering, we must create and sustain rituals that allow us to feel the connection we crave, while broadening rather than constricting the range of that connection. Countless recovering alcoholics find this ritual sitting in circles together to enact recovery day by day, and the voices of millions walking peacefully in the streets singing "We Shall Overcome" still ring. With mindfulness we can shed the rituals that are not really serving us and cultivate the ones that make space for us to be our wholehearted selves together, with no one left out of the infinite circle.

21. Art

Picture people absorbed in seeing, then taking a few slow steps to gaze at another painting in rapt concentration. Art museums create a context that invites us into mindfulness. People pour their attention into the works on the wall, and the works hopefully respond by being wondrous, or perhaps inspiring people's mindfulness. We don't really know. If a late-period Matisse was lying by a dumpster in an alley, how many people would walk on by? As the great poet Thomas Gray wrote:

Full many a flower is born to blush unseen,
And waste its sweetness on the desert air.

As you may have heard, Joshua Bell, one of the most accomplished violinists in the world, once went down in a subway plaza to play music. He played music by some of the greatest composers of all time on his Stradivarius. About a thousand people walked by, and about seven stopped to listen for a few minutes. He collected thirty-two dollars. A few days later he played a sold-out show at a major concert hall. I can picture people in that concert hall, eyes closed, transported by the glory of the sound, and I can see the oblivious folks marching by him on the way to work.

I've seen this firsthand. When I was touring as a musician I once found myself opening for a rock star with a big song on the charts. Everyone thought that since it was a major show I must be good, and though almost no one there knew who I was, fifteen hundred of them stood in pure attention as I played my set, which they punctuated with applause. A couple weeks later I played a coffee shop, where no one had much expectation for the music. I played the same set, but folks were just reading the paper, coming and going. There was no notice when I would end a song and start another. But you know, I have played music outside a subway platform, and though no one paid much attention, it was wonderful. Playing music is something I love to do, something that calls forth all of me into the present moment: my heart, my mind, my senses, my body.

Have you ever had a profound experience with a work of art while you weren't paying attention to it? I suppose it might have happened and we would never know, but I do suspect that at some time, or maybe countless times, you have found yourself powerfully moved and completely engaged with a song, a dance, a movie, a story, a painting, or a poem. We may be looking at something already made, hearing something being created at this very moment, or creating something ourselves, but it draws us deeply into the moment, and it happens because of some ineffable relationship between ourselves and this thing we call art. There is intimacy there for us, but we do have to pay attention.

It's so good to give our attention to great works of art. They show us new ways of seeing, and they help us realize our connection to others, to understand people we think are so different. They can show us truths we might otherwise miss, and they bring us beauty. If we see beauty, if we give our attention to beauty, it will enter us and be a part of us, and we will be a little more likely to create beauty. Listening to Duke Ellington's music may not turn you into a musical genius, but it increases your ability to create in your own way. Some-one once asked Bob Dylan in an interview long ago who his influences were, and he replied that you open your ears and your eyes and you're influenced. What you pay attention to will change you.

To offer yourself to the possibility of seeing things anew through art is to open up to the infinity of our connections. Picasso's paintings challenge the way we see the world and open up new ways of seeing, but his work, so singular and visionary, was rooted in African sculptures and masks. Experiencing someone's art can give us a flash of insight into the life of a person who might be different (and yet not so different) from ourselves, whether it's the poetry of Langston Hughes or Gwendolyn Brooks, or the paintings of Frida Kahlo, or a Japanese haiku. On her piano, my mother used to keep the sheet music for John Cage's *4'33"*, a three-movement piece of music, four minutes and thirty-three seconds long, where no sound is created by the musician. I've performed it a few times. People like to laugh at this composition, but through it I have learned that there can be music everywhere, in a concert hall or in the kitchen: the purr of air conditioning in a quiet meditation hall, the songs of birds and breezes, my voice in song accompanied by the loud, clear sustained note of a vacuum cleaner as we clear the dust from the floor.

You don't have to be good at making art, and you don't have to be smart to enjoy it. Just jump in. Find things that move you, and find things that are sort of hard to understand but might stretch you. Don't forget to enjoy that weird little drawing your niece made. Mindfulness and attention will nurture her ability to feel intimacy. They will show you the beauty that comes both from making something the best you can and from sharing it.

22. Food

Somewhere in one of the few remaining places where hunter-gatherers can still live their ancient, right-now way, a hunter is thanking an animal he has slain. Somewhere a child is delighted with a bowl of steaming rice. Someone is chewing on a sandwich as they scroll through pages on their phone. Someone is sweating in a broad field of green and loam, hand-picking fruit from a vine. Like the air we breathe, food is absolutely central to our ability to be on this earth. Like the air we breathe, food can be a wonderful invitation into the present moment and our interdependence.

In the West we tend to be pretty alienated from our food. It's easy to eat lots of food in heavy packaging, made of components from all over the world, many of which are chemicals that we can't even pronounce, let alone know what we're eating them for. I suspect lots of city folks eat beef who have never even seen a cow alive and in the flesh, not to mention seeing one being slaughtered. We get a little closer to our food when we cook, when we hand-chop vegetables and combine them ourselves in a sizzling pan. I've heard growing your own food is even more intimate, but to be honest I haven't tried it. I have volunteered in the garden at a Zen center though, and there's something that feels just fundamentally good about cutting a bunch of fragrant basil off the stalk, washing it in a bin, chopping it up, and making some pesto to serve to friends. Kids have a reputation for not liking healthy food, but kids I know who work in a summer garden love to eat those vegetables they grow.

Many people have difficult relationships with food: eating too much, not eating enough. This can be extreme, and people die from unhealthy eating and eating disorders. This is too big of a topic for this book, and certainly if you have a lot of distress around food, I hope you find some help and support to take care of it. If you are looking for a healthier relationship with food, mindfulness can be a part of the healing path. Focusing compassionate, nonjudgmental awareness on feelings, thoughts, and actions related to food and eating may help soften harmful habits and open up your capacity to decide on and enact a way that feels better.

Valuing food is embedded in traditional cultures. Families organize get-togethers around it. People pray for it: "Give us this day our daily bread." It isn't always easy to get food, and every day hundreds of millions of people go without enough. A lot of folks, however, never have to worry about going hungry, and it gets pretty easy to take food for granted. How many people at this very moment are eating food for which they have no sense of gratitude, toward which they feel almost no connection, and which they are hardly experiencing as they eat? It's easy to relate to food this way, and our culture supports us doing it. We are given the message "You *deserve* a break today": drive through here and get food handed to you by a nearly invisible person, which you can eat as you drive to do something else. A lot of food is intimately connected with systems of violence. Vast numbers of animals are killed for human consumption, and raising these animals has an enormously disproportionate impact on the warming of our planet and depletion of habitat for other living beings.

We are not, however, victims of culture; we are a part of it. We can be mindful of it and we can participate in our own way and thus help shape it. The Soto Zen tradition in which I train and teach has a wonderful food culture that has helped shape my life and the way I eat and cook. In a Soto Zen temple one of the main officers, and one of the most important spiritual positions, is that of head cook, or *tenzo*. Planning meals and cooking food, activities so basic to human life, are not thought of as low or secondary to spiritual practice, but rather are exalted and fundamental. You may picture a Zen master floating on a cloud of wisdom in the mountains, but really they are probably carefully slicing a mushroom for some soup. This is a reminder that when we're in the kitchen making food, it's worth it, and it's wonderful to just devote all our energy to the task at hand. We don't have to wait for some more important part of our lives or more important project to show up for us to fully live.

Eating and serving food is also handled with reverence and attention in Zen. Temple meals are served in a beautiful ritual called *oryoki*. Each aspect of the meal—serving, getting out one's bowl, eating, and cleaning up—is done with precision. This precision is an invitation into mindfulness, total attention to the experience. To really give your attention to any moment is amazing, and food really highlights this. I've had people give me effusive praise for rice I cooked for them on retreat: plain white rice that they might have barely noticed or not bothered to eat at a restaurant, that we might find ourselves shoveling down at home while reading a magazine. Honestly, I'm not that great at making rice, but a moment of real attention yields astonishment.

During an oryoki meal there are several chants. They focus on acknowledging great exemplars of virtue and wisdom, and all the people, plants, and unknown beings who are a part of our great fortune to be able to have a meal. They call to mind our intimacy with all of life. In these chants we ask that all the benefit of our eating may be for the whole world, for everyone and everything. We don't claim to know how that's going to happen, but if we acknowledge our intimacy with the world and ask that what we receive be for the benefit of everyone, something good happens. If nothing else, something happens to our hearts. Softening our sense of entitlement and desire, and cultivating our sense of gratitude and giving, frees us from our aloneness and brings us into connection.

Practice: Mindful Eating

Countless cultures show wonderful ways to cultivate and express this connection at mealtime. I encourage you to be mindful of your own habits around food and, with the awareness you find, to see what serves you and what you might want to change. You can create your own way, connected to everyone else's way. And be mindful of just the simple act of eating, of making food. If you're eating alone, put away the phone and the book and just eat and see what happens. If you're with others, just pause here and there and give your whole attention to the raw sensations of eating, the aroma of a hot soup rising in steam, the feel of crusty bread cracking between the teeth, the sweet, sharp tang of orange on the tongue.

23. Community

Take a breath. This is air you share with everyone. Read these words. How many people were involved in bringing them to you? I don't know, but I'll say thanks to all the people at Wisdom Publications and the kind woman I talk to at the warehouse when I order books. Who made the paper or encoded the ebook? We don't know. Who helped them get their boots on when it was cold and they were small and had to go to school? We don't know, but these people are all part of our community. Ultimately, whether we know it or not, and sometimes whether we like it or not, we are involved in a worldwide community of intimate connection. There may be people we'd like to think are outside of our group, but they are still part of the vast unfolding that allows this moment to be how it is.

We develop our feelings and ideas about community early in our families, in schools, at churches, and on playgrounds. We'll carry these formative views throughout our lives, and we change and evolve as well. I watch people at the Zen center where I teach: Some hover around the edges for a long time; they'll tell me, "I'm not a joiner." Others dive in and want to be a part of everything, never be left out. There are countless variations. Whatever your relationship to community is, it's OK. It's good, however, to bring some mindfulness to your attitudes. Take some time to think about communities you've been part of or avoided, and just be aware of how you feel about them, what thoughts tend to arise. It's good to do this because human beings are naturally social, so our sense of community has a big impact on our lives. And it's also good to do this because we're already an intimate part of many communities as well as the one whole community of the world. It's good because it helps us to understand this intimacy and do our part of it with some joy and an open heart.

I walk through my neighborhood and see a bunch of twenty-somethings strewn about a front porch, talking, laughing. Then in the park I see a big family with a grill smoking, children chasing each other beneath the bushes, grandparents sagging into big canvas chairs, and folks fussing over food. A flock of ravens high up in the trees flits and dives in singles, pairs, and groups, voices chattering, calling, abating, arising. Dogs in the dog park chase and course in packs while one sits gazing on. Being together is part of the deal. Many years of evolution form this impulse to connect. I've seen a flock of geese chasing mallards off their territory. Ravens too—in chorus diving on a young owl hunched over a fresh-killed rabbit, until the little owl's food fell to the ground to be subsumed in a black, writhing crowd of birds. I've seen a room full of human beings dumping all their anger and frustration on another group. When our sense of community hardens, we lose sense of the unknowably vast, soft boundary of our place in the community of all of life.

So, yes, it's good to be mindful of our thoughts and feelings about community. Are we afraid to be a part of one, afraid we will be engulfed? Do we want to hide ourselves inside one and be safe and absorbed there? Ultimately it's good to be comfortable in community and comfortable in your own skin. Once we have some sense of predilections, we can open up to our feelings and find ways to soften our fears and aversions. Afraid of being alone? Practice doing it. Avoidant of community? Test the waters by stretching and spending time in a group. Test your edges. No need to go too far, just play with your life. See what happens.

We are part of many kinds of communities: families, groups of friends, neighborhoods, religious groups, cities, states, nations, ethnicities, political groups. They overlap here and there, and here and there they don't. Our sense that we are part of these communities can help us feel supported and connected, but if we really want to know and live from the deepest sense of intimacy, we need to cultivate our sense of being part of the infinite community of life.

The web that connects us all is endless, but we can't see it. When you put on your pants in the morning you (probably) can't see the person's hands who sewed the seams. When you throw a piece of plastic in a trash can, you can't see the person who will dump it in the landfill next week. It is good to cultivate awareness of just how many people's efforts go into providing you the things you use throughout your day. We are supported by so many people at every moment. This community is truly amazing. If you watch the TV news you may think that the world is full of horrible problems—and this is sort of true—but the human race is constantly involved in an astonishingly harmonious effort to support each other, which we rarely acknowledge.

Intimacy, however, is not just about realizing how good it is to be close. It includes all the difficult parts of our relationship. If we want to have an authentically intimate relationship with our loved ones, we need to acknowledge the problems in our relationships. If we want to really deepen our intimacy with the community of humans on this planet, we need to deepen our knowledge of the harms that are part of this intimacy. In the United States many of us wanted to think that racism was over, but the vastly disproportionate number of black people in prison, the segregation of our cities, the enormous economic and educational disparities, and the shooting of unarmed black men have shown us that hiding from the truth of the persistence of racism in our country has only allowed it to fester. Some of us may be privileged enough to be able to think that racism is someone else's problem, but we are all part of the community—black, white, privileged, disadvantaged—and we all have our own unconscious biases around race.

Racism is only one of many painful and harmful aspects of our community that we are already intimate with but may want to hide from, or blame on someone else. Climate change, economic exploitation, homophobia, human-caused species extinction, rape culture, Islamophobia—the list is long. I'm sorry if this seems harsh, but this book is not about finding an intimacy that's magic and takes you away. This book is about mindfulness, awareness of what's here now, and real intimacy—intimacy that is brave and strong and can face all the truths of relationship. If we build up our capacity through mindfulness and intimacy with our bodies, minds, and hearts, we can be strong enough to truly face our intimacy with all the pain and harm in our communities. We can realize that it feels good to be real and to begin to orient our lives to taking care of everyone in our community, to taking care of everything. The activist and professor Cornel West said, "Never forget that justice is what love looks like in public." The love he is talking about is based on realizing the totality of our connection: Martin Luther King Jr.'s "inescapable network of mutuality."

If we want to live this way, we need to listen. Listen to the voices in your communities. Here I'm focusing on listening to voices in the big human-world community. Listen to people who are different from you, who have different views, different races, different lives. Use your mindfulness practice to help you hear. Reading is good too. Read with an open mind and awareness of your reactivity. Practice honoring and respecting voices that challenge your own view. These voices are part of your community; they are a part of you. You may want to believe the person you deem racist to be totally other than you, but realize they are still part of your community. If you want to promote everyone's welfare, they are going to be part of the process. If someone is challenging you, pointing out your prejudiced or privileged view, your complicity in our climate's destruction, can you employ mindfulness to truly hear them? They are still part of your community, and nothing you can do can wrest you from your intimacy with them. Whether we make each other enemies or not, we are all still in this together.

And here we are, standing at the door of the grocery store, thinking, "Yes, I am intimate with this vast, complex web that includes infinite love and support and vast, complex systems of oppression and destruction. What do I do now?" There is no easy answer. Intimacy is not about easy answers, but we can be mindful of what we're doing right now and do it with some care.

We can learn about ways large and small that we can live compassionately within our growing awareness of the completeness of our connection to both the most beautiful and the cruelest aspect of our community. Don't try to save the world. Open your heart, listen, and make one small beneficial step. Then do it again.

24. The Ones We Love

The teachings in this book are rooted in the idea that our thoughts, feelings, and actions come from our past conditioning, and that we can participate in this process of conditioning so that who we are and what we do flows in a more compassionate, joyful stream. Rather than making big dams and bringing in giant dredges, we might move a few rocks here and there, make a channel for the water to flow, or free a log that's pinned against a rock to find its way downstream. To open up to our intimacy with aspects of life we want to hide from, let's try not to be controlling and forceful. It helps to build on the firm foundation of our feeling of intimacy with the people and things we love.

We all have some sense of intimacy, of love. Perhaps with some people, or a person, perhaps with an activity, an artist, a religion, a god, or values like kindness, love, and peace. This sense of intimacy shows up in how we think, in how we feel, and in how we act. Many of the teachings in this book have been about deepening our awareness of how this sense of intimacy shows up. But here I encourage you to choose someone—or if someone seems too hard, something—with which you feel a strong sense of connection and love and be mindful of what that relationship feels like, and how it shows up in your actions. Remember, mindfulness should not include judgment or correction. This isn't about figuring out whether you are doing it right; it's about knowing what it's like for you to experience intimacy.

Practice: Mindfulness of a Loved One

Sit in an upright position with the body still and visualize the beloved. As the mind drifts, just continually return attention to this image.

As you do this, notice how you feel, and be aware of whatever thoughts arise. Try to let the thoughts go as you notice they are sweeping you away and return to the image of one you love.

This is a practice of mindfulness, of compassionate awareness of what it's like to focus on someone you love. It might also feel good to focus on someone you love while wishing them well. This is an ancient and powerful meditation practice.

Practice: Loving-Kindness Meditation

Loving-kindness meditation (also known as *metta* in Pali, *maitri* in Sanskrit, or friendliness meditation) is a wonderful way to both know how we feel about intimacy and to cultivate our capacity to experience it. Here is an abbreviated version of metta practice. More comprehensive teachings on this are wonderful and worth seeking out if you find this supportive. Like the meditation described above, focus the mind on an image of someone you love, and then slowly repeat these phrases in your mind:

> May you be happy.
> May you be healthy.
> May you be safe.
> May you be at peace.

When you notice the mind has swept you away, just return to the image of the beloved and the phrases. It's best to say each phrase with an exhalation; this helps us find a good pace for saying the phrases and ties it to the great source of all meditative approaches: mindfulness of breath in the body. As these words and this image flow through the mind, be aware of how you feel. Many people find this feels warm and wonderful, but it's not uncommon for difficult feelings to arise. If they do, it's OK. You are strong enough to be there with those feelings; just offer them your intimate attention and know that they, like all things, will pass away.

———————————————————

Doing this practice will help you to know, both consciously and unconsciously, what it is like to realize intimacy. It will build on the strength of your existing sense of connection. This practice opens the door for your growing sense of intimacy with all of life, and your ability to live from this sense of connection in a natural way.

25. The Ones We Don't Know

Many old Buddhist teachings say that seeing our inter-dependence is seeing truth, and not seeing it is igno-rance. Ignorance basically means not knowing. If you think about all the things you don't know—how many pins are in your pincushion, how many stars in the sky, how many people laughing within a mile of you and how many crying, how things are for each of the approximately forty trillion bacteria living as part of your body, where you left your umbrella, what's going on in Yemen right now or on Mars—you get the idea: we're pretty ignorant! It's all right, let's start there. Let's just take a moment to be intimate with the vastness of our ignorance, like a great ocean of not-knowing. Do you know what each of the billions of fish in the sea are experiencing right now? Intimacy with this not-knowing situation can open the door for a deeper sense of our interdependence and connection to what we can't know but are already a part of.

Usually we ignore what we don't know. The human mind picks out a tiny, infinitesimal corner of reality and tries to figure it out, and then spends a lot of time feeling like it's got a handle on things. Really it's ignoring infinite things to give itself a tenuous sense of security in the vastness of this wild, unfurling world. If we practice mindfulness of our body, mind, and heart, we can begin to see the process by which the mind constructs this small picture of the world. We see that our awareness moves between a broad, spacious sense and a constricted, narrow view based on how our body, mind, and heart are interacting. If we practice objectless meditation, the mind's categorizing slows and we tend to actually experience gaps in the mind's tendency to actively ignore most of what is happening. We find ourselves occasionally resting in a total nondifferentiated awareness. While we will always remain in a kind of ignorance about the infinite aspects of the universe, we can diminish the degree to which we actively, though generally unconsciously, ignore things. This is the path by which we begin to see interdependence, to see a world that is not made of things to judge, control, and manipulate, but a world with which we are intimate and to which we can offer our best effort.

Mindfulness and objectless meditation help us to work with ignorance, by helping the mind to shed its divisive tendencies, by letting go of our stories, ideas, and judgments. But we can also harness our mind's conceptual capacity to deepen our sense of interdependence, to ignore less and know more. All kinds of knowledge can be wonderful, but if we want to open up to intimacy, one of the best ways is to learn about people, animals, and nature. Our sense of intimacy is rooted in our early human relationships, and this is the base from which it is good to build. Think about all the people in your neighborhood you don't know; now extend this to the people in the neighborhoods you never visit, to other cities and rural areas, to other countries. These people all have a full human life as you do, and carry sufferings and joys just as you do. Can you find ways to connect to and learn about these people at the level of the heart? We tend to ignore people outside of our culture and normal milieu, and we barely know it. Many people have admired Jesus Christ for a very long time. He told his followers, "what you do for the least of these, you do for me," because he knew how easy it is for us to ignore those around us, particularly those who are suffering.

Practice: Mindfulness of People We Don't Know

To realize interdependence, seek out ways to connect at the level of the heart with people you don't know: people of other races, religions, economic situations, political beliefs, nations, and continents. Reading about people can be good, but even better is actually reading what they themselves say, hearing them say it. You can make this connection just by paying attention; a conversation isn't necessary, although it is wonderful if it's possible. It's great to go to a neighborhood where most people speak a different language or have a different shade of skin and just participate: go for a walk, go into a shop or restaurant, enjoy a church service or some music. Listen to radio or watch video that lets people you don't know tell their stories. Saint Francis wrote a prayer that says, "Let me seek to understand rather than be understood." You don't need to explain yourself; just listen, pay attention. Rather than ignoring, we can engage in the act of knowing. If we suspend our judgment, if we bring compassionate awareness, we will naturally begin to sense our intimacy.

I love to practice mindfulness and intimacy with animals. When I first started meditating I was working as a bike messenger in Minneapolis. Each day I'd head down to Loring Park and practice meditation by the pond until my first work got called in. Birds in profusion lived complex and dynamic lives right before my eyes. They fished, they darted about, they fought and groomed, they herded their young around. Squirrels and rabbits zipped here and there; they chased each other, they begged me for food. I didn't have any food for them, but we had our lives together. We were close. I didn't name them, I didn't become an expert on animal behavior, but I loved them, and I still feel, even now, a deep kinship with animals, just carrying on their lives as best they can, like me. I feel a deep gratitude for our shared time on this earth, and cherish the opportunity to enact my life in a way that does not harm them or their children's future, but keeps this earth a home for us all.

26. The Ones We Don't Like

At the end of the story of Little Red Riding Hood, the young girl and her grandmother are saved, and the wolf is killed. At the end of *The Merchant of Venice*, a young couple is joyously united and Shylock, a Jew, is forced to convert to Christianity and give up all his possessions. Countless Hollywood movies end with a couple's kiss and a villain expelled, killed, or lampooned. Deeply embedded in human consciousness, in our stories and our culture, is the idea that intimacy and union are deeply connected to the expulsion of a supposedly evil or merely alien other. On the other hand, many of the greatest spiritual leaders of all time have made the inclusion of everyone into the circle of love central to their teaching: Jesus Christ, Buddha, Rumi, Dr. King, Teresa of Avila, Abraham Heschel, Mother Teresa, Desmond Tutu, and so many more. These people have proclaimed and enacted a vision of a world that leaves violence behind. They did so by learning how to be nonviolent and encouraging nonviolence in others. I have a hunch they weren't perfect, no matter what the stories say, but their hope and their commitment are a beacon in the night.

When we consider someone else to be evil, at fault, or beyond the pale, our consciousness is trying to let us off the hook. Our judgment of others affirms our sense of being right and focuses on blaming the problems of the world on something or someone else. This actually disempowers us; as long as we're blaming the world's problems on something else, we're distracted from the opportunity we have right now to offer something beneficial. Ultimately, it is also painful to hold others at bay. The anger, hatred, and judgment that arise when we separate ourselves in this way are unpleasant to experience.

The tendencies to disagree with the weather, to hate another state's sports team or a particular singer, to hate a type of book or your ex-spouse or people of another political persuasion or people who do certain kinds of crimes or world leaders who cause harm—all exist on a continuum of expulsion in our minds. We experience them, with varying degrees of emotional intensity and verbal rhetoric, as alien, as other, as nonintimate. This tendency is extremely powerful and basic to being human, so it is extremely important to not make it, like all those things I just listed, an enemy. It is an intimate part of who we are, and if we'd like to let it fade and shed its power to create suffering, compassionate awareness will be much more effective than judgment and control.

When people are overwhelmed by suffering, it doesn't help to explain this view. What's best is to express it by embodying it. When a young woman who has been sexually assaulted (as one in five women in the United States have been) comes to me for spiritual support and is intensely angry toward her assailant and our culture, which supports sexual violence against women, it would be cruel and foolish for me to talk about the idea that she is connected to the attacker and the culture. I believe the best I can do in a situation like this is to stay present and compassionate toward her feelings. I try to avoid making the raised voice, the agonized tears, and the bitter speech an other; I do my best to stay there and include her whole expression in a field of compassionate awareness, to give her space to heal, and to let my intimacy with her pain transform me. When I was treated for posttraumatic stress disorder, first I needed to express and experience the whole range of related emotions in a safe space. Then, from being with the truth of my experience, my capacity for intimacy grew. When I see a video of people rioting in the streets, I believe my job is to stay present to the anguish and rage, not to judge how they express their pain and anger. This makes space for my actions to arise from a compassionate sense of connection, rather than abstract judgments or feelings.

Human consciousness makes "others." It makes them such that we talk behind our siblings' backs in judgment, and it can be so powerful that huge groups of humans arm themselves and engage in mass killings. It is important to respect the awesome power of this tendency, but it is also important to acknowledge just how massively destructive it can be, and step up as individuals and work to liberate ourselves. We can practice letting go of this habit and slowly build our ability.

Practice: Mindfulness of People We Don't Like

A great place to start is with people whom we just find mildly irritating—perhaps a colleague you'd rather avoid, or a waiter who is kinda grumpy, or a family member you love but who gets on your nerves. When you think of them or see them, just remind yourself that they want to be happy and well, just like you, and they are not perfect, just like you. Then see if you can pay attention to them just how they are when you meet them; notice and let go of whatever story you're bringing into the situation about the past or the future. Be mindful of your emotions; notice how it feels when you're around them. Notice how these feelings change, especially, if you come back to seeing your shared desire for wellness and your shared imperfection.

I haven't met anyone who has done this who hasn't reported a decreased amount of suffering and an increase in good feelings about how they are acting. Try it out! Then you can begin to employ it with folks whom you find more troubling. See what happens.

I recall when I first learned this approach to dissolving my need to make a "disliked other." The United States had a president I hated. I would turn on the news and drive to work and swear whenever I heard his voice or what he was doing. But I decided I was tired of getting to work all angry and worked up. So I didn't turn the radio off, but when I heard him talking, I'd think about our shared humanity, our basic need for wellness, and our shared brokenness. I'd just listen to the sound of his voice, and I'd notice how I felt. After a while, I felt no animosity toward that human being. However, I still felt that I could help the world by working against his reelection, and I put a bunch of time into volunteering to get someone else into the presidency.

Many of my greatest heroes are those who have endured incredible harm but emerged without hatred and with enormous energy to work for the greatest possible good: Nelson Mandela, Mahatma Gandhi, Sister Chan Khong. Jailed, exiled, having seen beloved members of their community killed, they remained focused on doing what would heal the world and let go of hatred. Think of all the healing and power the Dalai Lama and Desmond Tutu have been a part of, and all the joy they show while doing it. We can't expect anyone to do this, but we can be inspired to follow their example. We can be the change we want to see in the world.

People sometimes say to me that it is anger that drives their engagement with healing the world, helping the downtrodden, and this may be true. All things, however, are intimately connected, and anger hurts. I don't claim anger is bad or wrong; I just know that it is painful. If you love the world enough to work for liberation, I hope you can love yourself enough to want to be free from this pain. I believe there is nothing you can do motivated by anger that you cannot do better motivated by love.

27. The All

In an ancient story, the Buddha comes back to the forest from his morning walk to town to beg for his day's food, and after eating he offers to teach the gathered meditators everything. He says, "I will teach you the All." Imagine their excitement! Their beloved teacher is going to lay it *all* out. He says if you want to create true peace you must know the All. And what, he asks, is the All? Sight, sound, smell, taste, touch, and thought. Simply what is here in your own direct experience right now. You already have what you need to walk the path of peace, of wellness, of nonsuffering. You don't need to wait until you are a better person, or have a different job, or get a degree, or have time to meditate, or get done meditating, or have a new wife, or your kids move out, or, or, or … You don't need to wait. It doesn't mean you won't suffer; it just means that right here in your five senses and mind is your opportunity to do something beneficial.

Here's good advice, often attributed to Mother Teresa: "Be faithful in small things, because it is in them that your strength lies." When we focus on this moment of our senses and mind, we bring things down to a workable scale where we can find our true strength. One of the highest and most revered offices in the Soto Zen tradition is that of cook. The head cook should be a person of deep, sustained practice, and the practice of cooking for the community is profound. The cook expresses practice by giving full attention to lining the fingernails up along the edge of a carrot to protect the fingertips from the slicing knife, giving wholehearted attention to an assistant who is not sure how to toast sesame seeds, putting their whole heart into planning a day's meal that will be simple and healthy for a group of meditators devoted to taking care of their lives as they are.

I'm sure Mother Teresa had her flaws, but her achievements in promoting human welfare are amazing, beyond knowing. Can you measure the impact on the world of thousands of people being cared for, of millions of people being inspired? If you and I wait to act until we can pull off what Mother Teresa has done, we may find ourselves still on the couch till well after dinnertime, and perhaps for the rest of our lives. This is only true, however, if we forget her advice. We can focus on the small things, just as she did. We can stick to what's here right now, the All.

To call this moment of experience you are having *the All* may seem wrong. What about the farthest galaxies and the young children I don't know on the other side of the world? Where are those in this "All"? Thinking of this moment of experience as All has two implications: it's all you've got to work with in terms of doing something beneficial, and since everything is always infinitely, intimately connected, it is your window to everything. The first of these is intimately related to mindfulness. The teachings on the All remind us that you can't really do something yesterday or tomorrow; you can only act now. Right now, you can plan to do something tomorrow, and it might happen, but ask anybody honest and you'll hear that some of those things we're going to do tomorrow don't happen. What we're doing now is always what we are actually doing. Mindfulness is about bringing your heart and your mind to what's here. It is about finding the ground of your true empowerment, this moment of experience, this "All."

The second implication of these teachings on the All is about intimacy. Since all things are already interconnected, this moment really matters. When you shout angry words through the closed window at another driver from your car, where does the harm end? You suffer, and your mind and actions are conditioned to suffer in a similar way again. The person you've shouted at is likely to be stressed. Other people who see the event will feel this stress as well, and it will manifest in how all of you drive, and show up at work, and greet your children, who are deeply impressionable and will absorb this pain and find it creating patterns in their hearts and minds. When you smile at a checkout clerk, walk peacefully in solidarity with an oppressed group, or carefully take off your shoes when you come into your house, a whole different kind of effect is sent out into the All, is offered to your moment of experience and its infinite connection to everything.

You have all that you need to give your effort for the good, the true, and the beautiful. You are already aware of this moment. Can you let yourself rest in knowing that the whole world comes together in this moment of sight, sound, smell, taste, touch, and mind? What is here for you? What small thing can you offer?

Acknowledgments

This book comes from infinite sources; no one can own it, but I am grateful to have been part of its life. I am indebted to so many great Buddhist teachers, in particular Gautama Buddha, Mahapajapati, Patacara, Vasubandhu, Shitou, and Dogen Zenji. The intimate transmission from teacher to student, upheld for millennia, so fully embodied by the great nuns Xinggang and Yikui, and generously shared by my teacher Tim Burkett, carries my writing forward. I have also sought and been carried by more recent inspirations: Ida Wells, Mahatma Gandhi, Dr. King, Malcolm X, Black Elk, bell hooks, Thich Nhat Hanh, Harriet Tubman, and Dorothy Day. Too many surely to list. In this writing, where I have erred, I own it, and where there is good may we see it as only a riffle in a great river of love.

I acknowledge that I live on land taken from Dakota people and carry countless unearned privileges due to my light skin, male sex, European heritage, and middle-class upbringing. I pray that knowing this may help me be humble and open to change.

To everyone at Wisdom Publications, and particularly the gifted Laura Cunningham, editor of all the books I've written: bows.

To Tomoe Katagiri for her time by my side practicing one stitch, one stitch, one stitch, and for intimately passing on Buddha's robe: bows.

I have been blessed to share in the intimate practice of Zen with many dear friends at Minnesota Zen Meditation Center. You are too many to name, but some have walked the path with me so kindly for so long: Bussho Lahn, Susan Nelson, Kimberly Johnson, Ted O'Toole, Guy Gibbon, Wanda Isle, and Rosemary Taylor. A bow to you.

Without a thousand friends in addiction recovery with hands outstretched, I would not walk this earth, and without the many wonderful psychologists who've walked with me, that walking would be fraught with ancient pain. I humbly hope this book carries your compassion forward, and honors your path of practice. A deep bow to you all.

No one taught me more about being human than my dear family of birth: my mother, father, and brother. It is from you, at the very root, that I learned and learn to love.

I have no greater inspiration than my children and stepchildren: Max, Rocky, Daisy, Finn, and Delaney. May you find freedom in the bonds of love.

I am so grateful to share the loving intimacy, the daily and nightly truth of being who we are, in joy, in sorrow, in sleeping, and in waking, with my dear Colleen.

Selected Bibliography

Bodhi, Bhikku. *In the Buddha's Words: An Anthology of Discourses from the Pali Canon.* Boston: Wisdom Publications, 2005.

Bodhi, Bhikku. *Middle Length Discourses of the Buddha: A Translation of the Majjhima Nikaya.* Boston: Wisdom Publications, 1995.

Caplow, Florence, and Susan Moon, eds. *The Hidden Lamp: Stories from Twenty-Five Centuries of Awakened Women.* Boston: Wisdom Publications, 2013.

Dogen, Ehei. *Moon in a Dewdrop: Writings of Zen Master Dogen.* San Francisco: Northpoint Press. 1995.

Dogen and Kosho Uchiyama. *How to Cook Your Life: From the Zen Kitchen to Enlightenment.* Translated by Thomas Wright. Boston: Shambhala, 2005.

Easwarn, Eknath, trans. *The Dhammapada.* Tomales, CA: Nilgiri Press, 1985.

Ferguson, Andrew. *Zen's Chinese Heritage: The Masters and Their Teachings.* Boston: Wisdom Publications, 2011.

Fromm, Erich. *The Art of Loving.* New York: Harper and Row, 1956.

Gunaratana, Henepola. *Mindfulness in Plain English*. Boston: Wisdom Publications, 2015.

Hanh, Thich Nhat. *Peace Is Every Step: The Path of Mindfulness in Everyday Life*. New York: Bantam, 1992.

Hanh, Thich Nhat. *Understanding Our Mind: 50 Verses on Buddhist Psychology*. Berkeley, CA: Parallax, 2007.

hooks, bell. *All About Love: New Visions*. San Francisco: William Morrow, 1999.

hooks, bell. *Feminist Theory: From Margin to Center*. Cambridge: South End Press, 2000.

King, Martin Luther, Jr. *A Gift of Love: Sermons from "Strength To Love" and Other Preachings*. San Francisco: Harper and Row, 1963.

Leighton, Taigen Dan. *Cultivating the Empty Field: The Silent Illumination of Zen Master Hongzhi*. Clarendon, VT: Tuttle, 2000.

Lorde, Audre. *Sister Outsider: Essays and Speeches*. Berkeley, CA: Crossing Press, 2007.

Manuel, Zenju Earthlyn. *The Way of Tenderness: Awakening through Race, Sexuality, and Gender*. Boston: Wisdom Publications, 2015.

Murcott, Susan. *First Buddhist Women: Poems and Stories of Awakening*. Berkeley, CA: Parallax, 1991.

Okumura, Shohaku. *Living by Vow: A Practical Introduction to Eight Essential Zen Chants and Texts*. Boston: Wisdom Publications, 2012.

Stevenson, Bryan. *Just Mercy: A Story of Justice and Redemption*. New York: Spiegel and Grau, 2015.

williams, angel Kyodo, Rod Owens, and Jasmine Syedullah. *Radical Dharma: Talking Race, Love, and Liberation.* Berkeley, CA: North Atlantic Books, 2016.

Willis, Jan. *Dreaming Me: Black, Baptist, and Buddhist: One Woman's Spiritual Journey.* Boston: Wisdom Publications, 2012.

Yang, Larry. *Awakening Together: The Spiritual Practice of Inclusivity and Community.* Boston: Wisdom Publications, 2017.

About the Author

Ben Connelly is a Soto Zen teacher and Dharma heir in the Katagiri lineage. He also teaches mindfulness in a wide variety of secular contexts including police and corporate training, correctional facilities, and addiction recovery groups. Ben is based at Minnesota Zen Meditation Center and travels to teach across the United States. He is the author of *Inside the Grass Hut: Living Shitou's Classic Zen Poem* and *Inside Vasubandhu's Yogacara: A Practitioner's Guide*. He lives in Minneapolis, Minnesota.

What to Read Next from Wisdom Publications

INSIDE VASUBANDHU'S YOGACARA
A Practitioner's Guide
Ben Connelly
Foreword by Norman Fischer

"Through Connelly's luminous teaching, some of Yogacara's most vivid and inspiring innovations come to life… Newcomers and adherents to this lesser-known Buddhist school alike are lucky to have Connelly as an exceptional guide to the central themes of Yogacara."
—*Publishers Weekly* Starred Review

INSIDE THE GRASS HUT
Living Shitou's Classic Zen Poem
Ben Connelly
Foreword by Taigen Dan Leighton

"The very essence of Zen."—Mike O'Connor

UNSUBSCRIBE
Opt Out of Delusion, Tune In to Truth
Josh Korda

"Josh Korda makes Buddhism relatable and fresh, weaves in neuroscience and psychology, and serves it all up with a heaping dollop of candor, fearlessness, and wit. This book is a how-to guide for people wanting to learn how to face demons, forge deeper connections, sit comfortably in their skin, and step away from the distractions of social media and mindlessness of consumerism—things we all know will never leave us satisfied. Tune in and unsubscribe."—Cara Buckley of *The New York Times*

SANCTUARY
A Meditation on Home, Homelessness, and Belonging
Zenju Earthlyn Manuel

"Zenju Earthlyn Manuel's *Sanctuary* offers us much-needed clarity and light in a time of increasing violence and confusion, daily assaults on our basic sense of belonging. Here is a generous feast of wise and compassionate insights into the deeper meanings of homelessness and home, identity and community, refuge and liberation. This is genuine and nourishing food for the challenging journeys ahead." —Acharya Gaylon Ferguson, PhD, Core Faculty, Naropa University

Living Mindfully
At Home, at Work, and in the World
Deborah Schoeberlein David

"Simple, direct, and full of real-world wisdom, Deborah's excellent new book is for everyone interested in bringing mindful awareness into their daily lives."
—Susan Kaiser Greenland, author of *The Mindful Child*

About Wisdom Publications

Wisdom Publications is the leading publisher of classic and contemporary Buddhist books and practical works on mindfulness. To learn more about us or to explore our other books, please visit our website at wisdompubs.org or contact us at the address below.

Wisdom Publications
199 Elm Street
Somerville, MA 02144 USA

We are a 501(c)(3) organization, and donations in support of our mission are tax deductible.

Wisdom Publications is affiliated with the Foundation for the Preservation of the Mahayana Tradition (FPMT).